steve sonderman

NO REGRETS STUDY SERIES

MEN WITH NO REGRETS

Live Life on Purpose and Impact the World

Beginning Your Mission with God

NO REGRETS STUDY SERIES

Book 8:
Beginning Your Mission With God

Published by No Regrets Men's Ministry
Elmbrook Church, Inc. | 777 South Barker Road | Brookfield, WI 53054
www.menwithnoregrets.org

Distributed by:
NextStep Resources | 7890 12th Ave South | Bloomington, MN 55425
1-800-444-2665   www.nsresources.com

© 2016 by Elmbrook Church, Inc.
All Rights Reserved. No part of this publication may be reproduced, stored in a retrieval system, or transmitted in any form or by any means, electronic, mechanical, photocopying, recording, or otherwise, without the prior written permission of the publisher.

Printed in the United States of America
ISBN: 978-0-9984764-7-6

"Scripture quotations are from the ESV® Bible (The Holy Bible, English Standard Version®), copyright © 2001 by Crossway, a publishing ministry of Good News Publishers. Used by permission. All rights reserved."

Scriptures taken from the Holy Bible, New International Version®, NIV®. Copyright © 1973, 1978, 1984, 2011 by Biblica, Inc.™ Used by permission of Zondervan. All rights reserved worldwide. www.zondervan.com
The "NIV" and "New International Version" are trademarks registered in the United States Patent and Trademark Office by Biblica, Inc.™

Visit us at www.menwithnoregrets.com

MEN WITH NO REGRETS   Beginning Your Mission with God

Welcome to the No Regrets Study Series

I do not know a man alive today that wants to get to the end of his life looking in the rear view mirror and seeing a long list of regrets.

The regret of being a passive father… The regret of a failed marriage… The regret of standing on the sideline… The regret of going through life alone… The regret of broken promises…

No, the men I know want to get to the end of their life and be able to say, like the apostle Paul in 2 Timothy 4:7, "I have fought the good fight, I have finished the race, I have kept the faith." The men I know seek to live life with a purpose, participating in something bigger than themselves to make an impact on the world around them.

My guess is you are no different. Deep down, your desire is to live with No Regrets too; to be the fully alive man God created you to be. You may just need a little help getting there. This, my friend, is exactly why I wrote the *No Regrets Study Series*. This is a Bible study series just for you, the man who longs to be a Godly servant in his home, church, workplace, community and world. This is a series written to help you be a champion where it really matters – in the eyes of God, your wife, children, and friends.

As you work through this series together with your small groups, follow hard after Christ and begin to live your life on purpose. I promise you your life will never again be the same. God is going to take you on the adventure of your life!

For the Cause that Counts,

Stu

Steve Sonderman
Associate Pastor Elmbrook Church
Founder, No Regrets Men's Ministries

Contents

About the Author	4–5
Introduction	6–7
Lesson One – Everyman: Made for Mission	8–18
Lesson Two – The Story?: God's Mission for the World	19–33
Lesson Three – Your Mission: Move Out into The World	34–41
Lesson Four – Join with God: Discover your Mission	42–56
Lesson Five – It's Game Time: The Man God Uses	57–71
Lesson Six – The Mandate: Go Make Disciples	72–83
Lesson Seven – Practical Principles: How to Invest in Eternity	84–94
Lesson Eight – Life Plan: The Man with No Regrets	95–109

Resource Section

Small Group Covenant	112
Small Group Job Roles	113
Spiritual "Vital Signs" Self–Assessment	114–115
Personal Spiritual Conditioning Goals	116
Accountability Questions	117
Scripture Memory Secrets	118–119
Guidelines of Reading Old Testament History	120–121
Small Group Prayer Requests	122–125
No Regrets Men's Ministries Resources	126–131

www.menwithnoregrets.org

About the Author

Steve Sonderman

Steve Sonderman realized in college that God was calling him for full-time ministry. Soon after turning his life over to Christ, he began his ministry leading home Bible studies for the local area high school students. After earning his degree in Education from the University of Wisconsin–Milwaukee, he headed up to Bethel Seminary in Saint Paul, Minnesota where he received his Masters of Divinity.

Since 1984 he has been an Associate Pastor at Elmbrook Church in Brookfield, Wisconsin beginning with leading the College–Age Ministry. In 1992, Stuart Briscoe called him to start one of the first Men's Ministries in the country for the growing church congregation. Since then he has grown a vibrant ministry serving thousands of men weekly.

Knowing that every man longs for a sense of purpose, a chance to participate in something greater than themselves, Steve teaches men that living with No Regrets means serving God, family, church, community and their entire circle of influence. Believing that God's plan is to take every man that follows Him on an adventure of a lifetime, he has dedicated his life to empowering men to get out of the pews and follow Jesus.

Steve's real passion is to see every local church have its own ministry to men. He is the founder of the *No Regrets Men's Ministries*. In 1995, he began the annual No Regrets Men's Conference which today draws over 6,000 men to the live event. Recently the conference has expanded even further with a live feed of the event available to churches and men's groups around the country. Steve regularly consults and leads seminars in this country and around the world with churches from a wide range of denominations helping to develop and establish local men's ministries and address leadership issues. Working with both pastors and leaders of men, he has been called to help train "men who disciple men who disciple men".

In addition to the No Regrets Study Series, he is the author of *How to Build a Life–Changing Men's Ministry* and the newly published *Mobilizing Men for One–on–One Ministry* as well as several Bible studies written exclusively for men.

Steve and his wife, Colleen, have successfully raised four grown children. They have recently become empty nesters and appear to have happily transitioned into this new phase of life. Steve and Colleen enjoy taking walks with their 130-pound Newfoundlander dog, Misha, dining out with friends and visiting their children across the country.

NO REGRETS CONFERENCE:
One Day, Multiple Sites, One Purpose

WE STREAM IT. YOU HOST IT.
MEN'S LIVES CHANGE.

Host the No Regrets Conference at your local church by live video stream. We stream the music, speakers, and other life changing content. You choose to pick up the entire day or add your own live seminars and music.

For more details, visit www.menwithnoregrets.org

Introduction

How to Get the Most Out of Your Small Group Experience.

Your group is embarking on a life–changing journey. The No Regrets Study Series is a powerful study that provides breakthrough teaching about what it means to be a fully–devoted follower of Jesus. In order for you to get the most out of your next 8 weeks, it is important for you to be prepared each week. Your full participation will be crucial to the success of the group. Each of your members will play a vital role in and how your group functions. Let's take a look at what you can expect to do before class and together in class.

Before Class:

In order to fully engage each week and get the most out of the experience, you will need to spend time each day working on a section of the lesson. The homework has been divided into short daily segments. Each week you will do some of the following:

Bible Memorization – We recommend you write the verses out on a 3x5 card and keep them with you throughout the day so you can learn and review as you go. If you do not own a Bible, it is important that you get one for this study. We recommend a good study Bible such as the Life Application Study Bible, NIV Study Bible or ESV Study Bible.

Bible Study – Throughout the course of the series you will learn several Bible study methods including verse, chapter, topical, and character study.

Supplemental Reading – For each of the study guides there is a corresponding book that needs to be purchased. Most weeks you will be reading a chapter or two from the book and taking some brief notes.

Video/Audio Message – In a couple of the lessons there will be a video/audio message you will need to listen to and take notes on the page provided. To access the messages, go to www.menwithnoregrets.org and find *NR Study Series Resources*. Then enter Password: NRSS (uppercase letters). Videos are also available for purchase on DVD through our website.

Personal Reflection – In some lessons you will have a time of reflection on the various elements of your study that week. We have provided some questions and exercises so you can begin to apply what you have learned to your life.

Optional Homework – A number of weeks will offer optional homework. If you have the time, feel free to work through those. *Time Expectation: Most weeks will take you two hours to complete the work. We would suggest you try to work 15-20 minutes each day to spread it out over the week.*

In Class:

The group will meet weekly for one and a half hours depending on schedules. Make sure to bring your book to every class. The in–class time will be broken down into two basic segments: Small group sharing, accountability and prayer; and Large group discussion.

Getting Started (10 minutes) – This period should only take five to ten minutes. The two things you will do are open your time in prayer, and have a Bible memory verse review.

Small Group Sharing, Accountability, and Prayer (40–50 minutes) – After the opening prayer and memory verse review, you will break into groups of 3–4 men for small group sharing and prayer. We recommend you stay in the same group for the entire 8 lessons and then change groups for the next book in the series. There are questions in your study that will guide this time. Each man will decide where he wants to be held accountable by the group. Make sure to leave 10–15 minutes at the end of this section to pray for one another.

Large Group Discussion (40–50 minutes) – For the discussion both groups will come together and discuss the questions found in the study guide. The questions and exercises provided will encourage you to take all you have studied and worked on and incorporate it into every day life. You may not get through all the material, and that's okay. Each person should leave the group with one or two key principles they are going to apply to their life, or at least seek to apply in the coming week. Keep in mind the following guidelines for having a healthy discussion:

- **Be Involved** – Jump in and share your thoughts. You have a perspective that is unique and can benefit the other group members.
- **Be a Good Listener** – Value what others are sharing, try to understand their perspective, and don't be afraid to ask follow-up questions.
- **Be Courteous** – Always treat others with respect. When there is a disagreement, focus on the issue and never turn the discussion into a personal attack.
- **Be Focused** – Stay on topic and keep the side conversations to a minimum.
- **Be Careful** not to dominate the conversation – Be aware of the amount of talking you are doing in proportion to the other group members.
- **Be a Learner** – Come with a learning spirit each week and be sensitive to what God may want to teach you through the lesson.

taken from R12 Coach Study Guide, a resource from Fellowship of Christian Athletes

Close in Prayer – At the end of the discussion, someone will close the meeting in prayer. This prayer should reflect and respond to what God has done in your group during the session. You want to make sure that you finish on time to honor the time commitments of those in the group.

I am so excited for you to get started. I know God plans to do big things in your life as you surrender all and work to become fully devoted to Him. If you do the work and make an authentic commitment, this small group experience will be life changing. I'd love to hear your stories of transformation as God begins to work in your group.
You can contact us at **www.menwithnoregrets.org**

MEN WITH NO REGRETS Beginning Your Mission with God

LESSON ONE
Everyman: Made for Mission

Goals for the Lesson:
To understand that we have been made by God.
To begin to see that God is calling us to join Him in His mission for the world
To reconnect with your group and set new group accountability questions and recommit to the group covenant

As a young man, William Borden was heir to the Borden Dairy estate. He was a millionaire by the time he graduated from high school. As a gift on the event of his high school graduation, Borden was sent on a trip around the world. (I don't know about you, but I was given a typewriter for college.) Traveling throughout Asia, the Middle East and Europe, he experienced a growing concern for the hurting and lost of the world. He wrote home to say, "I'm going to give my life to prepare for the mission field." After making this decision, he wrote two words in the back of his Bible: "NO RESERVES."

From there Borden went on to Yale University with purpose and determination. During his first semester he began a campus wide student movement to meet regularly, read the Bible and pray. By the end of his first year, 150 fellow freshman were meeting for weekly Bible studies. By the time he was a senior, 1,000 out of Yale's 1,300 students were joining together in these groups. Beyond the campus, Borden founded the Yale Hope Mission to reach out to those on the streets of New Haven, Connecticut. All of this was set in the context of his call to foreign missions, which soon focused on Muslims in China. After graduation, Borden was offered numerous high-paying jobs, but he declined them all in order to pursue the mission field. At this point, he wrote down two more words in the back of his Bible: "NO RETREATS."

Borden next went to graduate school at Princeton Seminary, where he was ordained to the ministry. After he finished his studies, he set sail for China through the China Inland Mission, stopping first in Egypt to study Arabic. While there, he contracted cerebrospinal meningitis. In less than a month, William Borden was dead. He was twenty-six years old. But before his death, knowing that the steps of his life would take him no further, he had written two more words in his Bible; beneath "No Reserves" and "No Retreats" he had written "NO REGRETS."

William Borden understood that he was made for a mission and all of his life was going to be submitted to fulfilling that mission. It is no different for each of us. Each one of us has been made by God, and for God, and to join God in His mission for the world. Of all the studies, this one gets me the most excited, because there is something within each of us as men that desires to be a part of something bigger and grander then ourselves! Lesson by lesson we are going to examine what God is doing around the world and how we can join Him in it. In the end, I hope each of you will be able to say with William Borden, as for my life I desire to live with, "No Reserves", "No Retreat" and "No Regrets".

> *Many sincere Christians around the world are concerned for evangelism. They are delighted at evangelizing in their own communities and even in their own countries. But, they do not see God's big picture of "world need" and the "global responsibility" that He has put upon the Church in His world. The Christians in Nigeria are not to just evangelize Nigeria, nor are the Christians in Peru just the people in Peru. God's Heartbeat is for the World.*
>
> — Billy Graham

MEN WITH NO REGRETS — Beginning Your Mission with God

Before Class:
Memorize John 20:21.
Complete the Bible study on Jonah.
Read the excerpt, *Who Are We and What are We Here for?* from Christopher Wright's book *The Mission of God's People.*
A Time of Personal Reflection.
Optional: Listen to the Audio Message by David Wang entitled, *One Lord, One Name, One Call* (27 minutes).
To access the Audio message and excerpt, go to www.menwithnoregrets.org and find *NR Study Series Resources.* Then enter Password: NRSS (uppercase letters).

Day One – Memorizing God's Word: John 20:21

- This week you will be memorizing John 20:21. Write out the verse and begin to memorize it.

- In order to get its context read John 20.

For memory verse tips, review the "*Scripture Memory Secrets*" found in the Resource Section of this book.

Day Two – Studying the Word

Today you are studying the book of Jonah. It's a short book and a well-known story, but the background information below may give you some new perspectives on this prophet's story. In addition, there are four questions for you to answer. Make sure to read the **entire** book of Jonah before you answer the questions. (It takes about ten minutes to read through the book of Jonah.)

The book of Jonah is credited to the historical prophet Jonah, son of Amittai (2 Kings 14:25), who lived in the eighth century B.C., during the time of King Jeroboam II of Israel. While it is hard to pinpoint the actual date of the writing, we do know that these events took place when Nineveh was declining, but still the largest Assyrian city and notoriously wicked. We also know that Assyria had recently suffered through some attention-getting natural phenomena (a death-filled outbreak of plague and a complete solar eclipse), which could have affected the psychological stance of the proud Ninevites prior to Jonah's arrival. This book is different than other prophetic books in that it is not full of the text of Jonah's prophecies but, instead, focuses on his life. Little attention is given to what he actually said when he got to Nineveh.

Keeping in mind that the Assyrian Empire was one of the cruelest and most rapacious empires of the ancient world may help us to feel the impact of the word "Nineveh" to a pious Jew. For us, similar associations of disgust and terror might come at the mention of Hitler, Pol Pot, Stalin, Hutu/Tutsi, Khmer Rouge, Saddam Hussein, Chechnya, etc. It is also noteworthy that Jonah is the only prophet of Israel on record to be sent to a foreign country.

- Consider the following, you may sense three questions hanging over the entire book of Jonah. They are:

    1. What will Jonah do?

    2. What will Nineveh do?

    3. What will God do?

The Book of Jonah

- Reflection Question: Consider that Jonah said "No" to the directive from God that he should go with God's message to Nineveh. Have you ever said "No" to the challenge or opportunity to connect with "foreign" cultures? Cultures like: the inner city, those with differing political views, the elderly, the illiterate, the homosexual, the homeless, and the disabled.

- Thoughts:

- Reflection Question: In 2:9, Jonah is praising God for his deliverance, but then, when God extends this deliverance to repentant Nineveh, Jonah gets angry. Where do you see this attitude in the church today? How has judgmentalism or a sense of superiority hindered the advancement of the Gospel message? Do you have set notions about how it should look when someone "receives" Christ?

- Thoughts:

Everyman: *Made for Mission*

- Reflection Question: Where is the turning point in Jonah's attitude about his mission? How does the book of Jonah challenge our sometimes narrow views of God? How do we try to define God's calling in our own way?

- Thoughts:

- Reflection Question: Two hundred years ago, only 5% of the world's population lived in cities; now it is 50%. What impact does God's final statement in Jonah 4:11 have on your missional attitude? "Should I not be concerned about Nineveh, that great city?"

- Thoughts:

- Reflection Question: Any final thoughts on the Book of Jonah?

- Thoughts:

MEN WITH NO REGRETS   Beginning Your Mission with God

Day Three – Today you will be reading the first chapter from Christopher Wright's book, *The Mission of God's People*. The chapter is entitled, *Who Are We and What are We Here for?* To access the Audio message, go to www.menwithnoregrets.org and find *NR Study Series Resources*. Then enter Password: NRSS (uppercase letters).

Dr. Christopher J. H. Wright is International Director of the Langham Partnership International (John Stott Ministries in the US). He also chairs both the Lausanne Movement's Theology Working Group and the Theological Resource Panel of Tearfund, a leading Christian relief and development charity. He has written several books, including *The Mission of God and The God I Don't Understand*.

- Key Principles and Observations:

- What challenged you most from the reading?

- What were your favorite verses or quotes?

Day Four – A Time for Personal Reflection

Take a few minutes to work through the following questions and make sure to write a few notes on each. This is an opportunity to reflect on where you are at as you begin the final study.

In Isaiah 6, the Lord asks, "Whom shall I send? And who will go for us?" and Isaiah responded by saying, "Here I am. Send me." Have you ever come to the point in your life when you said, "Here I am Lord, send me?"

- As you look at your life, what has held you back from full surrender to God?

- What does it mean for you to join God in His mission for the world?

   · At work?

   · In your neighborhood?

   · In your community?

   · In the world?

- How have you been most challenged in your thinking and life this week?

- Where do you want to grow during the course of this study?

MEN WITH NO REGRETS Beginning Your Mission with God

Day Five – (Optional) Listen to the Audio by David Wang, entitled, *One Lord, One Name, One Call.* (27 minutes). To access the Audio message, go to www.menwithnoregrets.org and find *NR Study Series Resources*. Then enter Password: NRSS (uppercase letters).

David Wang, an expert on China, is a highly sought after speaker at international mission conventions and congresses. He has a God-given burden for China and keeps in close contact with the Church there. David comes from an affluent Shanghai business family. As a teenager, he went to Hong Kong and completed his education there. In 1966, David joined Asian Outreach, and led it into an outstanding pioneering mission in cutting-edge evangelism throughout Asia.

- Notes:

- Main Points:

- Primary Action Point for You:

In Class

Memory Verse Review – John 20:21

Small Group Sharing, Accountability and Prayer – 45 minutes
- Share your thoughts from Day Four's reflection, regarding where God may be calling you to expand your engagement with the world.

- Review the accountability questions listed in the Resources section of this workbook. Are there issues of accountability you need to restate so you are honest in where God is working in your life?

- Pray for each other that God would use your time together to enlarge your vision for engagement with the world.

Large Group Discussion – 45 minutes
- Discussion of the book of Jonah.
  - Do you have any culturally inbred biases that make you a bit like Jonah? Do you have a "Nineveh" – some sector of society that you would be unwilling or afraid to serve?
  - How is Jonah's response to God similar to peoples response today? How have we sophisticated and or rationalized not living out our "sent-ness" in the world?
  - How does the story of Jonah give you hope, especially chapter 3?
  - What do you learn about God's nature and character from this passage?

- Discussion of the reading, *Who Are We and What Are We Here For,* by Christopher Wright.
  - What challenged each of you the most from the reading? What questions do you have as a result?
  - How does Wright differentiate between mission and missions and missionaries?
  - Discuss the connection between the mission of the church and one's personal mission.
  - How will a man's life be radically changed and affected when he comes to the point of realizing and believing that he has been made to join God in His mission for the world?

MEN WITH NO REGRETS   Beginning Your Mission with God

Key Principles:
The Bible is our manual for understanding God's mission.
The arena for living out God's mission for the world is – the world of work, the public arena, the world of business, education, politics, medicine, sports and wherever else we live our lives.
God's vehicle to accomplish His mission is the Church. The Church was made for mission.

The Academy Award–winning movie Braveheart told the story of the Scottish freedom fighter William Wallace. Toward the end of the film, Wallace is in chains, awaiting his execution. On the strength of his passion and determination, he had led all of Scotland to revolt against their English oppressors. Time and again, his will and determination had bonded the spirits of the people into a force for national identity, pride, and freedom. But now he had been betrayed, handed over to his enemies, and sentenced to death. In the scene, a young woman urges the imprisoned Wallace to do whatever he can – regardless of its impact on his life mission or personal convictions – to stay the hand of his enemies, in order that his life might be spared. His response communicates one of the deepest truths of human existence: "Every man dies," he said. "Not every man really lives."

Men, you will never really live, unless you are willing to answer the call of God to join Him in what He is doing and wants to do in the world. This call is not necessarily a call to go across the ocean, but rather a call to see yourself as the hands and feet of Jesus wherever life takes you. To be missional in our living is to be other-centered rather than self-centered. Whether you realize it or not, you are the presence of Jesus in this world. Now we can spend the rest of this study learning what that looks like.

> *"Mission arises primarily out of the nature of God Himself; the living God of the Bible is a sending God. The Son sends as he himself was sent."*
> *– John Stott*

Looking for More about Becoming a Man of Missions?
The Mission of God's People, Christopher Wright
Holy Discontent, Bill Hybels
YouTube Video – *Sent: Living the Missional Nature of the Church*, Ed Stetzer
www.lausanne.org/en/multimedia/videos/ct2010-session-videos.html – Lausanne Conference on World Evangelization Message Series

LESSON TWO
The Story?: God's Mission for the World

Goals for the Lesson:
To understand God's Story from Creation to the New Heavens and Earth
To begin to understand your story in the context of God's Story — there is only one story and we are a part of it

In this lesson we are going to discuss the Biblical Foundation for Missions. The purpose is to convince us that world mission (the endeavor under God to bring the whole world to the feet of Jesus) is neither an unwarranted intrusion into other peoples' privacy, nor a regrettable Christian deviation, nor the hobby of a few eccentric enthusiasts, but a central feature of the historical purpose of God according to Scripture. Moreover, it is a responsibility which He lays (in some measure at least) upon all his people. It is no exaggeration to say that the Bible is a missionary book, because the God of the Bible is a missionary God. . . .

… where God calls Abram to be a blessing to "all the families of the earth". It is our prayer that these words, "all the families of the earth," may be written on your hearts. It is this expression more than any other which reveals the living God of the Bible to be a missionary God. It is this expression too which condemns all our petty parochialism and narrow nationalism, our racial pride (whether white or black), our condescending paternalism and arrogant imperialism. How dare we adopt a hostile or scornful or even indifferent attitude to any person of another color or culture if our God is the God of "all the families of the earth"?

> *We need to become global Christians with a global vision, for we have a global God.*
> *– John Stott*

MEN WITH NO REGRETS Beginning Your Mission with God

Before Class:
Read the excerpt, *People Who Know the Story They Are Part Of* from by Christopher Wright's book *The Mission of God's People*.
Complete the Bible study *The Story*.
A Time of Personal Reflection.
Optional: Listen to the Audio message *The Biblical Basis of Mission* by John Stott. (53 minutes).

Day One – Today you will be reading the second chapter from Christopher Wright's book, *The Mission of God's People*. The chapter is entitled, "*People Who Know the Story They Are Part Of.*" To access the message, go to www.menwithnoregrets.org and find *NR Study Series Resources*. Then enter Password: NRSS (uppercase letters).

- Key Principles and Observations:

- What challenged you most from the reading?

- What were your favorite verses or quotes?

Day Two, Three & Four – Studying the Word

There are many great stories in the world, but the greatest story of all is God's story. Before anything else existed, God was already here. He always has existed and always will. He is a wonderful and unique being to whom there is no equal. God is more beautiful and complex than anyone can understand. He is a mystery, but He has chosen to make Himself known. God's story is recorded in the Bible and as a Christian, knowing and understanding His story is very important.

I would encourage you to take a couple of days to work through the following passages that will reveal God's story throughout the Bible and time.

"The Story" Episode 1 - Creation

In the beginning, God made the world and everything in it. God took great care to create a world that would reflect his power and character. After forming the earth, God filled it with all kinds of plants and animals. Everything God made was good. God completed His creation by making human beings in His image, meaning they were not only good, but they were more like God than anything else He had created.

God made a man and a woman and he placed them in the Garden of Eden. They were able to talk to and receive instructions from God. They had nothing to hide and were completely comfortable in His presence. God told the humans to multiply and fill the earth and gave them the responsibility of ruling and taking care of the good world He had created.

- Read Genesis 1–2.
  What does this passage teach us about God?

What does it tell us about human beings?

What does this passage reveal about the world?

In Genesis 1:27, it says human beings are "created in the image of God". What does it mean to be made in God's image? How does this effect how we view people?

Key Concepts:
Everything God made was good
Humans have a role in God's creation – to multiply, fill and rule
Humans are more like God than any other creation
Both males and females are made in God's image

"The Story" Episode 2 - Rebellion

God encouraged the humans to eat from many trees in the Garden of Eden, but He commanded them not to eat fruit from the Tree of Knowledge of Good and Evil, warning that if they ate its fruit they would die. The serpent told the humans it was okay to eat fruit from the forbidden tree, causing the humans to question God's command and wonder if God was keeping the best things in life from them.

The humans believed the serpent's lie and chose to eat from the tree, rejecting and ignoring God's instructions in favor of going their own way. As a result of their sin, they experienced physical, emotional, relational and spiritual brokenness. The humans retained God's image and remained responsible for filling and taking care of the earth, but brokenness in the world made their role much more painful and difficult.

- Read Genesis 3

  What does this passage teach us about God?

  What does it teach us about human beings?

For many of us who have heard it several times, the story of the human beings "first sin" can begin to lose its power. But stop and think about it . . . the first human beings lived in a world with no brokenness. They had complete access to God. They could speak with Him. They had nothing to hide and were completely comfortable in His presence. Yet, despite all that, they still turned their backs on God.

MEN WITH NO REGRETS   Beginning Your Mission with God

- With such an incredible environment and relationship with God, why do you think the first humans turned away from God?

- In what ways have you seen this same story unfold in the world around you?

Key Concepts:
Spiritual, physical, emotional and relational brokenness entered the world.
The brokenness is profound and is spreading.
God's role for humans is still intact, but now much more difficult.
God's image in humans is marred but not lost.

"The Story" Episode 3 - Promise

Even though people had rejected Him, God did not turn His back on them. Beginning with a man named Abraham, God worked to raise up a group of people who would live in His ways and represent Him to the world. God showed Abraham and his descendants what He was like and how He wanted human beings to live. What started out as a small group of people eventually became a nation. God promised them a future king who would bring about reconciliation between God and humans, and fix the brokenness in the world.

These people of promise, Israel, would serve as God's voice by sharing His plan of restoration with others. They were to be living examples of Gods grace and love to those around them. Israel struggled to follow God, and more often than not chose to disobey him. The results were catastrophic, and brought further brokenness and chaos into the world.

- Read Genesis 12:1–4, Jeremiah 31:31–34 and Isaiah 43:10–12
  What do these passages teach us about God?

What do we learn about human beings?

Are there parts of this promise that are still in the future? If so, what are they?

In the Promise episode, human beings turned away from God over and over again, but God continued to pursue them anyway. Rather than seeing human beings as failures or beyond hope, God chose to make Himself known to them, to send His presence to be with them, and to initiate a plan to restore humanity to God.

Promise is by far the longest episode in the Bible, taking up almost the whole Old Testament. Here are a few of the highlights:
- Patriarchs – God calls Abraham and begins working in his family.
- Exodus – The people of God are miraculously delivered from Egypt.
- Conquest – God leads His people into the promised land.
- Kingdom – Israel lives in the land under David and many other kings.
- Exile – Israel disobeys and God causes them to be taken into captivity.
- Return – Israel is brought back to the promised land.

• God is still pursuing us today, how have you seen God pursue you?

Key Concepts:
God raises up a people through Abraham.
God's people are to live out the promise.
God's promise is not just for Israel but for all of creation.
Israel was to serve as God's voice.

"The Story" Episode 4 - Rescue

When the right time came, God sent Jesus Christ as the fulfillment of his promise. Jesus was both completely God and completely human. He always walked in God's ways. Many people failed to recognize who Jesus was and chose to reject and crucify Him. But what looked like defeat was all part of God's plan. Jesus rose from the dead, overcoming the powers of sin and evil.

The life, death and resurrection of Jesus paved the way for human beings to be reconciled with God and for the whole earth to be recreated and restored to its original unbroken beauty. Jesus life provided humans a model of how to live in God's way, His death paid the price for humanity's sin and rebellion, and His resurrection assures His people of their future hope.

- Read Hebrews 9:27–28, 2 Corinthians 5:16–21, Romans 3:21–26, and 1 Peter 3:18. What do these passages reveal about God?

What do these passages teach us about human beings?

MEN WITH NO REGRETS — Beginning Your Mission with God

How do the passages connect with the earlier parts of God's story?

Key Concepts:
The life, death and resurrection of Jesus changed everything.
Human sin and brokenness is redeemed.
Jesus' life gives us a model of how to live in God's way.
The resurrection ushers in the beginning of the new creation.

"The Story" Episode 5 - Restoration
After rising from the dead, Jesus ascended into heaven and sent the Holy Spirit to guide and empower His followers as they lived out God's mission of making all things new. Jesus' followers known as the Church, began living in radical obedience to God and sharing the message of Jesus everywhere.

God's people have the privilege and responsibility of joining in God's work of rescuing and restoring the world by telling others about Jesus and filling the earth with His love and justice. One day Jesus will complete His work by removing or refining all things until the original unbroken beauty of His creation is restored. God will return to live with His people forever in His renewed creation. The restoration of the world that began with the resurrection of Jesus will be extended to all of God's creation until God's will is done on earth as it is in heaven.

- Read the Following Passages: Revelation 21:1–8 and 2 Corinthians 4:16–5:5, 5:16–21. What do these Scriptures reveal to you about God?

What do these passages teach us about human beings?

MEN WITH NO REGRETS Beginning Your Mission with God

Where does your life need to be made new?

The final episode of God's story has already begun but is not yet completed. This is where we find ourselves in the story. At Jesus' resurrection, God ushered in a new era of restoration. We get to join in with what God is doing. This involves both sharing the message of Jesus with others so they can experience His redemption, and bringing all aspects of creation under God's rule.

Key Concepts:
God is making all things new.
The Church is one of God's main restoration vehicles.
All of creation will eventually be "on earth as it is in heaven".
Restoration culminates in a new heaven and new earth.

The Story?: *God's Mission for the World*

Day Five – Optional. Listen to the Audio message *The Biblical Basis of Mission* by John Stott (53 minutes). To access the Audio message, go to www.menwithnoregrets.org and find *NR Study Series Resources.* Then enter Password: NRSS (uppercase letters).

John Robert Walmsley Stott CBE was an English Christian leader and Anglican cleric who was noted as a leader of the worldwide Evangelical movement. He was one of the principal authors of the Lausanne Covenant in 1974. In 2005, he was ranked by *Time Magazine* as among the 100 Most Influential People in the World. He wrote over 40 books, the best known among them being *Basic Christianity*.

• Notes:

•Main Points:

• Primary Action Points for You

In Class:

Open in Prayer

Small Group Sharing, Accountability and Prayer – 35 minutes
- In your study this week you were reminded that God is in the business of making all things new (2 Corinthians 5:17). Share with the men what part of your life needs to be made new.

- Spend time praying for each other.

Large Group Discussion – 50 minutes
- Prior to doing your Bible study and reading this week, how relevant were the Old Testament Scriptures for your understanding of the church's mission? How has your view been changed and challenged this week?

- How did the reading by Christopher Wright and the Bible study complement each other and/or conflict with each other?

- We tend to explain the Gospel in the form of a series of propositions or doctrines. In light of the whole Bible story, as summarized in your study/reading, how would you summarize the Gospel in more narrative form? How does this effect how you share the Gospel with others?

- How have you been personally challenged this week as it relates to your mission in the world?

- How do you see the larger story of God reflected in your own stories?

Key Principles:
The story of God is a story of God's own mission.
Our story is a part of God's greater story, and we get to join Him in it.
To be a part of God's story brings responsibility and challenges.
The mission of God's people is vast and various.

"Our mandate for world evangelization is the whole Bible. It is to be found in the creation of God (because of which all human beings are responsible to Him), in the character of God (as outgoing, loving, compassionate, not willing that any should perish, desiring that all should come to repentance), in the promises of God (that all nations will be blessed through Abraham's seed and will become the Messiah's inheritance), in the Christ of God (now exalted with universal authority, to receive universal acclaim), in the Spirit of God (who convicts of sin, witnesses to Christ, and impels the Church to evangelize) and in the Church of God (which is a multinational, missionary community, under orders to evangelize until Christ returns)." – **John Stott, "The Bible in World Evangelization" in Perspectives on the World Christian Movement (ed. R.D. Winter and S.C. Hawthorne; Pasadena: William Carey Library, 1981).**

What we have seen this week is that God is on a mission and He has been on a mission from the beginning of time. It did not start with the coming of Jesus, but long before. It is seen from Genesis to Revelation. What is so amazing to me, is that He wants to include each of us in this mission. He desires you and me to join Him. Next week we are going to look at the world in which He is calling us to minister.

> *"The missional church then is a sent church. It is a going church, a movement of God through His people, sent to bring healing to a broken world."*
> – Michael Frost and Alan Hirsch, The Shaping of Things to Come

---

Want to Learn More About God's Mission:
Christian Mission in the World, John Stott
Mission of God's People, Christopher Wright
The Mission of God, Christopher Wright
Kingdom Come, Allen Wakabayashi
Audio message by Christopher Wright on the Mission of God:
http://missionsforum.wordpress.com/2011/11/30/chris-wright-on-the-mission-of-god/

MEN WITH NO REGRETS Beginning Your Mission with God

LESSON THREE
Your Mission: Move Out into The World

Goals for the Lesson:
To begin to see the world as Jesus sees the world
To better understand the world that we are being sent to

The world as we know it is currently a place of pain, brokenness, confusion, strife, and war. There is war in Pakistan, Syria, and many other countries. Fifteen million children are going to die this year due to starvation. Sex trade and human trafficking is destroying the lives of ten's of thousands of youth. Modern technology has brought many medical breakthroughs, but also has produced some of the most deadly weapons this world has ever known. AIDS, Malaria, and Influenza continue to spread killing millions yearly. The economic crisis of late has put a heavy burden upon every consumer and one wonders if we are in for a worldwide economic collapse. Is it any surprise that at the same time morality has plunged to a new depth.

And perhaps the greatest issue is that there are close to 7 billion people on the face of the earth today, yet close to 5 billion do not know Jesus! And if the Gospel is true, at this moment they are separated from God in their sin, and assuming nothing changes, will spend an eternity in hell – 5 billion people.

Everywhere you look you see a world spinning out of control and you wonder, is there any hope? How do we make sense of the world we live in and how in the world are we supposed to minister in it?

This lesson is designed to give you a little insight into the world that Jesus calls us to live and minister to. It is very easy as those living in the West to get very comfortable and to ignore the plight of the developing world. We can no longer turn our back as followers of Jesus. As we have seen in the first two lessons, God is on a mission to redeem the world, and He is calling you and I to be a part of it. As you begin this lesson, I would ask you to pray a very simple prayer, *"Father, allow me to see the world as you do."*

Your Mission: *Move Out into The World*

Before Class:
Memorize Luke 4:18 – 19 and complete the Bible study that goes with it.
Watch a couple of short videos from the Lausanne Conference on World Missions that took place in Cape Town, South Africa in 2010.

Day One – Memorizing God's Word: Luke 4:18–19

• This week, memorize Luke 4:18–19. Write the verses in the space provided.

• According to Jesus, what were the five goals of His ministry?

MEN WITH NO REGRETS   Beginning Your Mission with God

Day Two & Three
– Watch the Video messages from the Lausanne Congress on World Evangelism. To access the Video messages, go to www.menwithnoregrets.org and find *NR Study Series Resources*. Then enter Password: NRSS (uppercase letters).

The Third Lausanne Congress on World Evangelization (Cape Town, 16-25 October 2010) brought together 4,200 evangelical leaders from 198 countries, and extended to hundreds of thousands more, participating in meetings around the world, and online. Its goal? To bring a fresh challenge to the global Church to bear witness to Jesus Christ and all His teaching - in every nation, in every sphere of society, and in the realm of ideas.

Your assignment for the next several days is to listen to as many videos as they relate to the condition of the world. Most of them are between 5 and 15 minutes.
I would suggest the following to get started:
  · Tuesday October 19 – Pranitha Timothy – Human Trafficking
  · Tuesday October 19th – Richard Stearns – Wealth, Poverty and Power
  · Friday October 22nd – Tim Keller – God's Urban Mission

Then choose any other ones that look interesting to you as it relates to the condition of the world and use the notes section below to take notes on what you hear.

Video #1: Title: Speaker:
• Notes:

• Main Points from talk:

Your Mission: *Move Out into The World*

Video #2: Title: Speaker:
• Notes:

• Main Points from talk:

Video #3: Title: Speaker:
• Notes:

• Main Points from talk:

MEN WITH NO REGRETS   Beginning Your Mission with God

Optional Video #4: Title: Speaker:
- Notes:

- Main Points from talk:

Optional Video #5: Title: Speaker:
- Notes:

- Main Points from talk:

Your Mission: *Move Out into The World*

In Class

Open in Prayer

Memory Verse Review – Luke 4:18–19

Small Group Discussion – 40 minutes
- How has your study of the world this week challenged your view of mission and the world?

- What attitudes, biases, or prejudices need to be dealt with in your life to go wherever, and do whatever, God wants you to do?

- Each person pray a brief prayer asking God to increase their sensitivity to where He wants to mobilize them to meet the needs of the marginalized of the world.

Large Group Discussion – 40 minutes
- How are the poor of the Western world different from the Third World poor? How might the work of ministering the good news of Jesus to the marginalized of the West differ from ministering to the marginalized of the Third World?

- Discuss the messages you listened to from the conference at Cape Town.
    · What were the main points the speaker made?
    · How was your vision of the world enlarged or challenged?
    · Is there an action step for you?

- Did anyone listen to any optional messages? Share the main point the speaker made.

Close in Prayer.
- Pray for the poor who exist on the fringes of societies around the world. Let the Spirit guide your prayers of compassion for your fellow men and women – and especially the marginalized children – of the world.

Key Principles

Though fallen in nature, humans are no less valuable to their Creator than we ever were.
By deciding to identify with humanity as He did in the incarnation, the Creator shows how seriously He takes human beings.
God's heart is for the poor of the world.
How you regard or disregard the distress of the marginalized is a measure of your alliance with their Creator.

Bob Pierce was an extreme version of post–WWII evangelicalism: entrepreneurial, energetic, independent, and out to evangelize the world. In 1947, the young Youth for Christ evangelist started toward China with only enough money to buy a ticket to Honolulu. That was how things were done in Youth for Christ: God's work overcame all obstacles, and God's workers should "burn out, not rust out." Pierce eventually made it to China, where thousands came to Christ during four months of evangelistic rallies. Hunger was everywhere; communism hammered at the door. A compassionate Pierce was hooked. "My father went to China a young man in search of adventure," his daughter Marilee Pierce Dunker would write. "He came home a man with a mission."

Pierce later wrote haunting words in the flyleaf of his Bible: "Let my heart be broken with the things that break the heart of God." Dragging a movie camera across Asia – China was soon closed – Pierce showed the resulting pictures to church audiences in North America. He asked for money to help children. He showed their faces and begged Christians to "adopt" one. In 1950 he incorporated this personal crusade as World Vision.

In 1959, journalist Richard Gehman wrote that "[Pierce] cannot conceal his true emotions. He seems to me to be one of the few naturally, uncontrollably honest men I have ever met." When asked by Franklin Graham how to "shake people out of their complacency," Pierce said he had "become a part of the suffering. I literally felt the child's blindness, the mother's grief. … It was all too real to me when I stood before an audience. … It's not something that can be faked." Pastor Richard Halvorsen wrote that Pierce "prayed more earnestly and importunely than anyone else I have ever known. It was as though prayer burned within him… Bob Pierce functioned from a broken heart." — *Taken from an article by Tim Stafford, Imperfect Instrument*

Your Mission: *Move Out into The World*

Men, we live in a broken world, with the consequences of sin all around us, across the street and around the world. May our prayer be the words that haunted Bob Pierce, "Let my heart be broken with the things that break the heart of God." When we get up in the morning until we hit the pillow at night, may God continue to give us a vision and passion for the world in which we live. Next week we will start working on what that means for each of us.

> *"Let my heart be broken with the things that break God's heart."*
>
> – Bob Pierce, World Vision founder

Want to Learn More About God's Heart?
How to Be a World Christian, Paul Borthwick
2020 Vision, Bill and Amy Stearns
The Missions Addiction, David Shibley
World Christians, Sunder Krishnan
Perspectives on the World Christian Movement, Ralph Winter and Steven Hawthorne
Companion to the Poor, Viv Gregg
Cry of the Urban Poor, Viv Gregg

MEN WITH NO REGRETS Beginning Your Mission with God

LESSON FOUR
Join with God: Discover your Mission

Goals for the Lesson:
For each man to understand he has been made by God, for God, in order to join God in His mission for the world

To begin the process of discovering where you are going to join God in His mission

Over the past several weeks you have seen that from the beginning of time God has been writing a story, a story that started with creation, and included the fall. Christ came to rescue and restore. Some day He will come again to make all things new. But we have also seen that until He comes, our world is living in darkness and this darkness is evident in every segment of society and in every corner of the world. It is possible to look at the world and be overcome by anger and slip into passivity, because of just how overwhelming it looks. But God has a different perspective on things, and the God of heaven desires for us to join forces with Him, to join His mission for the world. This is exactly what these next couple of lessons are going to be all about. We are going to discuss how each one of us can discover our role as participants in the Mission of God. No matter where you live, what your age may be, or what you do for a career, God is calling each one of us as men to join Him in His Story to bring healing and hope to the world. We will begin connecting the daily work of our hands to God's great work of redemption.

As Bill Hybels says in his book *Holy Discontent*:
"And it is in this reality that what is enslaved can still be set free, what is broken can still be mended, what is diseased can still be restored, what is hated can still be loved, what is dirty can still be made clean, and what is wrong can still be made right... In other words, by knowing and walking with Christ, people can be freed from anything that has them tangled up. It was true for first-century believers, and it remains true for us today.

So here we go men, in this lesson you begin to discover where God may be calling you to join Him, and then in the next lesson we will talk about the type of man God uses to change the world.

Join with God: *Discover your Mission*

Before Class:
Memorize Acts 20:24.
Listen to the Audio message by Pete Briscoe, *What's On My Heart (38 min)*.
Complete the Bible study and accompanying exercise.
Spend time in Personal Reflection.

Day One – Memorizing God's Word: Acts 20:24

- Read this week's memory verse, Acts 20:24. Write out the verse below.

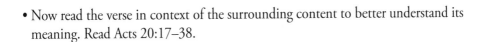

- Now read the verse in context of the surrounding content to better understand its meaning. Read Acts 20:17–38.

- Spend some time beginning to memorize the verse.

MEN WITH NO REGRETS   Beginning Your Mission with God

Day Two – Listen to the Audio message by Pete Briscoe from the book of Nehemiah. To access the Audio message, go to www.menwithnoregrets.org and find *NR Study Series Resources.* Then enter Password: NRSS (uppercase letters).

Pete Briscoe was born in Kendall, a small town in North England into the ministry family of Stuart and Jill Briscoe. Pete completed his undergrad work at Bethel College in St. Paul, Minnesota, and his Masters of Divinity from Trinity Evangelical Divinity School in 1992. Shortly before finishing school, Bent Tree Bible Fellowship in Dallas, Texas, invited Pete to join them as senior pastor, and he has served in that role since 1992. With a passion for God's Word and expositional preaching, Pete has led a church expansion in which membership has grown ten-fold. Bent Tree recently completed an extensive expansion that allows it to minister to more of the community. When not at work, Pete and Libby are busy raising their three amazing children, Cameron, Annika, and Liam.

- Notes:

- Main Points:

- Primary Action Points for You:

Join with God: *Discover your Mission*

Day Three – Complete the Bible study

Throughout the Bible there are many men and women who have lived with a sense of mission. They have understood that God has them right where He wants them and no matter what their vocation, God's desire is that they join Him in what He is doing in the world. For your study today you are going to read a number of passages of Scripture to get a sense of how God called them to the mission He had for them. This is not to be an inductive Bible study, but rather a reflective reading of several passages. I would encourage you to take notes along the way and see what God says to you through the process.

There are four potential studies—Moses, Gideon, Paul, Joshua. **You can choose which two you want to do for your study.**

The Call of Moses - Exodus 2:11 - 3:15

• How do God's heart and the heart of Moses break over the same thing?

• What was God already doing that He called Moses to join Him in?

• How did Moses resist the call?

- How do you see yourself in this story?

- What do you learn about discovering your mission from this passage?

Here is what Bill Hybels says about this encounter in his book, *Holy Discontent*: "Suffice it to say, the bush-on-fire tactic worked, Moses cooled his jets, and God got the chance to be heard, I think his words to Moses went something like this: "Moses, I completely understand the rage you feel. I too have seen the misery of my people in Egypt. I too have head them crying out. I too have felt their anguish as they suffer. What you saw when the Egyptian guy was beating the living daylights out of the Hebrew slave, and what you saw and heard when the two Hebrew guys were so frustrated, angry, and hopeless that they started beating each other – I saw those things too! And for what it's worth, I hate the sorrow and suffering as much as you do! More, actually.

"I am so stirred in my spirit, Moses, that I've decided to intervene from heaven" God probably continued. "I have chose to rescue them, and I want to use you to help me! I've been looking high and low for someone exactly like you. If you will participate in my plan, then I will harness the internal firestorm that rages inside you and channel it into positive action – action that will help set my people free from their slavery.

I'm going to assign you to a specific role because I see that you are as stirred up on earth as I am in heaven about this issue. I can see what this is doing to you on the inside! I see in you a passion for your people. In your raw emotion, I see a man with tremendous capacity for activism – a man who refuses to stand by idly while his people are being so dreadfully mistreated. Your frustration can forge leadership mettle and fortitude in you, Moses, if you will let it.

Because God couldn't stand the Israelites' mistreatment either, He used what I call a "firestorm of frustration" that was brewing in Moses' soul to launch this unlikely leader into a prominent role that resulted in the nation of Israel eventually inhabiting the Promised Land."

The Call of Gideon – Judges 6:1-40

- What are the reasons that Gideon does not feel worthy of leading?

- What does God remind him of in this passage?

- What is God calling Gideon to do?

God is going to use Gideon, not because Gideon is such a great man, but to show the greatness of the God who called him. God is not limited by our weaknesses. Our limitations simply give Him room to demonstrate His power. If He were to call you to a great work, would you trust in His power and accept His call?

MEN WITH NO REGRETS   Beginning Your Mission with God

The Call of Paul - Acts 9:1-31, 11:19-30, 13:1-4

- What is the mission that Paul is called to?

- How did God use Paul's past for his present ministry?

- How did God use others to help him discover his mission?

- What other lessons can you learn from these passages?

The Call of Joshua: Numbers 13:17-14: 9, Joshua 1:1-18

- What did the Lord see in Joshua to give him this type of responsibility?

- What Promises did God give to Joshua?

MEN WITH NO REGRETS   Beginning Your Mission with God

- What do we learn about hearing God's call on our life?

Joshua had many skills and talents that helped him to function effectively as a leader. Yet those skills alone cannot explain his phenomenal success. Only God can. God's presence was unmistakably obvious, not only to God's people, but even to unbelievers. And that presence make all the difference in the world. As Joshua yielded himself to God's guidance God was pleased to use his life for divine purposes. God often spoke to Joshua and made sure he knew His will. Joshua meditated upon the words God spoke. Joshua knew that his life and the lives of his countrymen, depended upon his understanding and obeying God's Word.

Join with God: *Discover your Mission*

Day Four – Reflection and Circle of Influence Exercise

From our previous studies, we have been reminded that God has always been involved in the world, whether in creation, delivering the nation of Israel, or sending Jesus to rescue us from our sin. He has never been absent from it or what is taking place in our world. The incredible thing about it, is that He has choose to take the initiative and involve His people with Him. He chooses to work through them to accomplish His purposes. It was true in the times of the Bible and it is true today. He is still using ordinary men like you and me to do His work here on earth. In this exercise you will take a few minutes to reflect on who God has brought into your life, where your circle of influence might be, what experiences and relationships you have had in the past and where you see God working around you.

- Key Relationships: Make a list of the people in your life: at work, club, team you coach, neighborhood, church, family.

- Circles of Influence: Begin to categorize by what area of your life you interact with them. Are they mainly at work, in the neighborhood, a club, etc.

Join with God: *Discover your Mission*

- What experiences and relationships have you had in the past that might be preparing you for what God wants to do in your life in the future?

- When you look into your world, where do you see God at work and how might you join Him in that work?

In Class:

Open in Prayer

Memory Verse Review – Acts 20:24

Small Group Sharing, Accountability and Prayer – 40 minutes
• Share with the men what God said to you through your study this week.

• What is holding you back from fulfilling God's mission for your life?

• How can the men pray for you this week?

Large Group Discussion – 40 minutes
• Discussion of the Audio message by Pete Briscoe.
  · In Pete Briscoe's message, he mentions a number of key principles for discerning where God wants to use you:
    - Think about where God has placed you
    - Realize God sends us on normal days
    - Ask questions close to our heart
    - Listen carefully for words of brokenness
    - Allow yourself to feel what God is feeling
    - Ask God to use you to intervene
  · Discuss as a group how these principles are instructive and helpful. What might these look like in your lives?

• Discussion of the Bible study. Begin by finding which studies were covered by your group.
  · As you read through how God called Moses, Gideon, Paul and Joshua to join Him in His mission for the world, what were the common denominators?
  · How were these men's objections similar? How are they similar to the objections we have today?
  · In each story, how did God ask the man to join Him in what He was already doing? How was it consistent or inconsistent with who they were as a man?
  · What are some of the main lessons we can learn from this study?

• Discussion of your Mission.
  · Each man share what has been stirring their heart and where they see themselves joining God. See the next page for a list of examples:

- Rallying resources for widow and orphan care
- Comforting grief-stricken people
- Helping men to break addictive behavior
- Fighting racism in this city
- Providing shelter for the homeless
- Working to solve extreme poverty or HIV/AIDS
- Fighting injustice in the world
- Helping Christ-followers get plugged into a small group
- Providing financial training
- Helping lost people find Christ
- Serving the needs of the under-resourced in the community
- Discipling new believers
- Ministering to those in prison
- Stopping human trafficking

• Moving Forward
  - Discuss as a group some practical things each of you can do to either discover where God wants you to join Him, or to start to get involved.

MEN WITH NO REGRETS Beginning Your Mission with God

Key Principles:
We were made for mission.
God wants us to join Him in his mission for the world.
We are to look for where God is working and join Him.

We were made by God for mission, and God is on a mission to restore the world and He asks us to join Him in the work. The Bible is full of men who answered that call: Nehemiah to rebuild the walls, Moses to lead the nation of Israel from slavery, Jonah to go to Nineveh to preach the Gospel, Paul to take the Gospel to the Gentiles, and the list goes on and on. The real question is not what each of these men in years gone by did, but what you are going to do today. No matter what your vocation might be, God desires each of you to live out your faith wherever you are, and to join Him in the work He is doing across the street and around the world. So, what is it for you, what is the firestorm of frustration that is burning in your soul? What will motivate you to get up in the morning, and keep you up at night? Men, next week we are going to talk about the type of man that God uses to make an impact in the world.

Before I formed you in the womb I knew you, before you were born I set you apart; I appointed you as a prophet to the nations.

– Jeremiah 1:5

Want to Learn More About Discovering Your Mission?
The Call, Os Guiness
Holy Discontent, Bill Hybels
A Work Heart: Understanding How God Shapes Spiritual Leaders, Reggie McNeal
Experiencing God: Knowing and Doing the Will of God, Henry Blackaby & Claude King

LESSON FIVE

It's Game Time: The Man God Uses

Goals for the Lesson:
To begin to grasp the truth that God can and wants to use all of us as men to influence our sphere of influence

To realize there are certain characteristics we can build into our lives that enhance our chance of being used by Him

Every team that is successful has one guy they go to in the clutch. When the game is on the line, when the pressure is on and the team needs a score or stop, this is the person they go to. In their glory years, the Bulls would go to Michael, the Packers go to Rodgers, Detroit goes to Verlander, the Lakers turn to Kobe, the Heat to D. Wade or LeBron, the Saints go to Brees, the Chicago Bears go to . . . really no one! One of the greatest examples I ever witnessed was Joe Montana in the Super Bowl between San Francisco and Cincinnati in 1989. Everyone in the huddle thought the same thing, "There he goes again. It is the Dallas game all over again." The San Francisco 49ers were down by three points with 3:20 left when Montana spotted–no, not an open receiver–but a personality. "There, in the stands, standing near the exit ramp," Montana said to tackle Harris Barton. "Isn't that John Candy?" And then he led the 49ers 92 yards, throwing for the winning touchdown with 34 seconds left. This was one of Montana's 31 fourth-quarter comebacks in the NFL.

The same is true in the spiritual realm as well. If you have not noticed men, the game is on the line. No matter what segment of society you look, at there are major problems and issues that need to be addressed, and God is on the search for that man who will be completely and totally available to be used by Him. This study is going to examine the type of man God will use to step up to the plate and make a difference.

MEN WITH NO REGRETS   Beginning Your Mission with God

Before Class:
Memorize Acts 4:13.
Complete the Bible study on the type of man God uses.
Spend time reflecting on the lesson, your life, your sphere's of influence.
Purchase your copy of *Transforming Discipleship* by Greg Ogden for the next lesson.

Day One – Memorizing God's Word: Acts 4:13

- Read this week's memory verse, Acts 4:13. Write out the verse below.

- Now read the verse in context of the surrounding content to better understand its meaning. Read Acts 4:1–22.

- How is this an encouraging verse to you?

It's Game Time: *The Man God Uses*

Day Two – Studying the Word: Christ's Ministry

For our study today and tomorrow you are going to look at six characteristics of the man God uses to influence the world around Him. The story of the Bible and history is that God specializes in turning ordinary men into "fearless" influencers of society. It always starts with a single man, wholly given to Him. In this study you will briefly look at what God is looking for in such a man. The study will revolve around the acronym IMPACT.

I - Intimacy with Jesus:

The principle we see all throughout scripture is the closer you get to Jesus, the greater the impact you will have for Jesus. One of the hardest lessons to learn is that our walk with Jesus is related to our work for Jesus, and unfortunately, oftentimes, the way we are doing the work of Jesus is actually ruining the work of Jesus in our own lives.

- Read through John 15:1 – 8 and Hebrews 12:1 – 3

- What does it mean to "Abide" in Jesus?

- What do you need to do to be consistent in your times with Jesus and to cultivate your private life? What is holding you back?

- It has been said that as men we settle for the barrenness of busyness at the neglect of our inner world. How has that been true of you and what do you need to do in order to counter that?

- Hebrews talks about the sins that entangle us and hold us back from running the race. What are those in your life right now?

It's Game Time: *The Man God Uses*

M – Multiply:

Ministry is about relationships, about investing your life into the life of others. The principle we see throughout all of scripture is that the closer you get to people, the greater the impact you will have in their lives. We see it in Moses investing in Joshua, Barnabus investing in Mark and Paul, Paul investing in Timothy and of course Jesus investing in the twelve. It was Dietrich Bonhoeffer who said, "The righteous man lives for the next generation."

- Read the following verses: 1 Thessalonians 2:8 – 9, 2 Timothy 2:2, Acts 1:8, Matthew 28:19 – 20

- What is the main theme of these verses?

- How is Jesus an example of living a missional lifestyle?

- What does it mean to be in the people business?

P – Prayer:

No matter what your education, your age, your job, you are able to pray. There is no greater power in the world than the power of prayer. If we are going to be used by God we must be men of prayer. God does not do any work other than through prayer. What God is looking for is men who are committed to, and dependent upon prayer. O'Hallesby, the great writer on Prayer says this, "The secret prayer chamber is a bloody battleground. Here violent and decisive battles are fought out. Here the fate for souls, for time and eternity is determined, in quiet and solitude. The greater the victory in the heavenly battle ground, the less blood will be shed on the earthly battleground."

- Read Matthew 9:35 – 38. What does Jesus ask the disciples to do? How does this relate to you and your ministry?

- Read Colossians 4:2 – 6. From Paul's prayer, what are some specific things we can pray for others?

- Who are the people you are praying for on a regular basis?

  · To come to Christ?

  · To grow in Christ?

  · To become a worker for Christ?

  · What missionaries are you praying for?

It's Game Time: *The Man God Uses*

Day Three – Bible study: Continue your study of the man that God uses.

A - Available:
Ian Thomas, the founder of the Torchbearers, ministry said years ago, *"It is not your ability, but your availability."* The glory of Christianity is its claim that small things really do matter and that the small company, the very few, the one man, the one women, the one child, are of infinite worth to God and are used by God for His glory. When one looks through the pages of scripture, you see over and over again, it is not the mighty that God used, but rather men who were available to Him. Availability is when you make yourself accessible for utilization. Availability is what we see in Isaiah 6:8 –
   "I heard the voice of the Lord, saying, "Whom shall I send and who will go for us?"' Then I said, 'Here am I; send me."

- Who are some of the men God used in Scripture that were simply available to Him?

- Read 2 Corinthians 12:8–10, 1 Corinthians 1:26–31. How do these verses support God's desire to use ordinary men to do the extra-ordinary?

- Read 2 Timothy 2:4. If we have no margin in our lives and are running from activity to activity, we will not have the time to get involved in the lives of others. Paul tells Timothy in this passage not to get so involved in civilian matters you do not have time for the work of the Lord. How do you need to build margin in your life?

> *"The world has yet to see what God will do with and for, and through and in the person fully consecrated to Him."*
> — *D.L. Moody*

C – Character:

Character is who you are when no one is looking. In a recent Gallop poll it was discovered the only difference between those who went to church and those that didn't when it came to ethics, how they spend their money, divorce, morality, etc. was where they spend one hour on Sunday, that was it! If we want to make a difference in the world today, it starts with who we are, our character.

> *"Nothing is more important in a leader's life and ministry than to lead an exemplary life in all things. Your leadership will be no more effective than your life. Your manner of living prepares the way for the reception of your words."*
>
> **– Wesley Duewel, Ablaze for God**

- Read Psalm 15 and reflect on its message.
  How does David describe what our character is to look like?

- Read through the following passages – 1 Timothy 3:1–10, 4:12, 6:11. When it comes to leadership in the church, what does Paul say we are to look for?

- Read Psalm 139:23–24. Ask the Holy Spirit to shine the light of His holiness into your life and convict you of where you are falling short. Where do you need to develop Christlike character?

It's Game Time: *The Man God Uses*

T - The Order of the Towel (Servant):

"Christian leadership in the future… is not leadership of power and control, but a leadership of powerlessness and humility in which the suffering servant of God, Jesus Christ, is made manifest… a leadership in which power is constantly abandoned in favor of love… Powerlessness and humility in the spiritual life do not refer to people who have no spine and who let everyone else make decisions for them. They refer to people who are so deeply in love with Jesus that they are ready to follow Him wherever He guides them." – **Henri Nouwen, In the Name of Jesus: Reflections on Christian Leadership**

- Read the following passages: John 13:2–17; Mark 10: 42–45.
  What instructions does Jesus leave with the disciples as it relates to serving others?

What did servanthood look like in the life of Jesus?

What are some practical ways that you can serve those around you?

- At work?

- At home?

- With your friends?

- In your neighborhood?

We are continually striving to create new methods, plans, and organizations to advance the church. We are ever working to provide and stimulate growth and efficiency for the Gospel. This trend of the day has a tendency to lose sight of the man. Or else he is lost in the workings of the plan or organization. God's plan is to make much of the man, far more of him than of anything else. Men are God's method.

> *"The church is looking for better methods; God is looking for better men. . . What the church needs today is not more or better machinery, not new organizations or more novel methods. She needs men whom the Holy Spirit can use—men of prayer, men mighty in prayer. The Holy Spirit does not flow through methods, but through men. He does not come on machinery, but on men. He does not anoint plans, but men—men of prayer!"*
>
> **– EM Bounds, Power through Prayer**

It's Game Time: *The Man God Uses*

In Class:

Open in Prayer

Memory Verse Review – Acts 4:13

Small Group Sharing, Accountability and Prayer – 40 minutes
• Share with the group a time that you made yourself available to God to be used by Him.

• What inconsistencies in your character do you see in your life that you need prayer for?

• Spend time in prayer for one another.

Large Group Discussion – 40 minutes
• When you think of the people that God used in your life, what are some of the qualities that stand out?

• Each man share with the group which Bible verse from the study had the greatest impact on him this past week.

• Discuss as a group what it means to be a person of influence. What does it look like in our world today?

• Discuss as a group how you can help each other: "Guard your Heart" Proverbs 4:23.

• Discuss what's next.

MEN WITH NO REGRETS   Beginning Your Mission with God

Key Principles:
It is not your ability but your availability.
Oftentimes our place of greatest use by God comes from our place of greatest brokenness.
God does not call the qualified, but qualifies the called.
God chooses to use the foolish, weak and ordinary of the world to do the extraordinary.

Oftentimes we are overwhelmed by a sense of insignificance. Don't you get the sense that many people feel they are an expendable commodity? They feel useless, like, "What can I do? I am just one and what can one do? What difference in the world can I make? What difference can I make at my school, work, neighborhood?" Some feel hopeless, while others feel helpless. Father Ted Hesburgh, President of Notre Dame for 35 years, says this, "*Our worst heresy is the belief that one life cannot make a difference.*" When I first heard that, I was stunned. After a quick look at history, it is obvious that our world has been changed by ordinary people like you and me.

1286 – A man by the name of William Wallace was fed up with the tyranny of the English, and went village to village all over Scotland to lead a revolt and free the country.

From 1787–1807 William Wilberforce worked tirelessly in the House of Parliament to see slavery abolished in England.

A young Albanian woman left her home to pursue her vocation in East India, and for 20 years taught geography in Calcutta. Each morning on her way to work, she would see men and women in the gutters, homeless, destitute, and full of disease. She quit her job, rallied her former students, and set about to rescue men, women and children who had been rejected by the hospitals and who were literally dying in the streets. She started her own order, the Missionaries of Charity. Before her death in 1997, she had received the Nobel Prize, established orders in 126 countries with more than 550 houses for the poorest of the poor. One lady, Mother Theresa, used by God.

Martin Luther King Jr. became famous for what he could not stand. The racial oppression he saw all around him in the 50's and 60's ripped him apart. He could not stand the "White Only" signs on drinking fountains, bathroom doors, and restaurants. He couldn't stand the fact that blacks were pushed to the back of the bus; he wanted the lynching of black people to stop, he wanted segregation to stop, he wanted justice to be served, that kids might grow up in a different world than he did. He lived the rest of his 39 years with a passion to see a new civilization ushered in – one characterized by nonviolence, freedom and justice for all. He was awarded the Nobel Peace Prize in 1964, and then in 1968 his life was taken, but not his legacy.

In 1950, Bob Pierce was in Asia when he saw an orphaned child from the Korean War drop dead in a food line. When he investigated he found out that there was not enough food at the front of the food line. He went home to the US and gathered some of his more affluent friends in a room in LA and started World Vision, with the promise to get food to the front of the food lines around the world. In 2005, more than 100 million people in 96 countries received physical, social, and spiritual support. In other words there is food at the front of the food line.

Here again it started with one person who made themselves available to God. Are you willing to be that man? Guys, the game is on the line, and God is looking for a man He can use to turn the tide, to stand in the gap for Him.

> *Example is not the main thing in influencing others – it's the only thing.*
> — **Albert Scheitzer**

Want to Step Up and Be More Available to God?
The Man God Uses, Henry and Tom Blackaby
Holy Discontent, Bill Hybels

LESSON SIX
The Mandate: Go Make Disciples

Goals for the Lesson:
To understand the biblical mandate for making disciples
To see that no matter where I am, I can be involved in the mission of making disciples

Steve always dreamed of his own business and financial success. But more than that, Steve truly believed in his dream to have computers – personal computers – in every home and in every office, affordable to all. He knew that such technology placed in the hands of men and women, boys and girls, would revolutionize the world. So Steve took the step of establishing himself as chairman of a startup computer company. But before long he realized that, while he knew computers, for his dream to be realized, he would need someone who knew business. Wanting the best available CEO for his young company, Steve sought out none other than John Sculley, CEO of Pepsi-Cola, in order to convince Scully to leave his prominent position and run Steve's fledgling enterprise. Somehow, some way, Steve got the meeting. Sculley listened patiently to the young man's vision and, after several meetings, introduced the man sixteen years his junior to reality:

> *"Well, you'd have to give me a million-dollar annual salary, a million-dollar signing bonus, and a million-dollar severance package."*

Steve was taken by surprise; such figures were unthinkable. But his boldness had brought him this far, so he took a risk and said, *"Okay, you've got it. Even if I have to pay for it out of my own pocket."* *"Steve,"* Sculley replied, *"I'd love to be an adviser to you, but I don't think I can come."* Steve's head dropped, then after a long pause, he issued a challenge that pierced Sculley to the depths of his being. Looking Sculley in the eye, Steve simply asked, *"Do you want to spend the rest of your life selling sugared water, or do you want a chance to change the world?"* Because of that challenge, Sculley resigned from Pepsi-Cola and became CEO of Steve's visionary little company.

And the rest, as they say, is history. Young Steve was none other than Stephen Jobs, and his fledgling computer company was called Apple. Under Sculley's skillful leadership, Apple became one of the world's leaders in computer technology and pioneered the use of personal computers. Together, they really did change the world.

Two thousand years ago, Jesus looked the twelve disciples in their eyes and asked a similar question: Are you going to spend the rest of your lives "selling sugared water" or, in their case, fish, or "do you want a chance to change the world?" We all have our chance. During the course of the next two lessons, we will examine what it looks like for each of us to invest our lives in those in our sphere of influence.

> *"When you die, you will live on in two ways, in eternity with Jesus and in the men, women and children you influence for Jesus."*
> **– Steve Sonderman**

MEN WITH NO REGRETS   Beginning Your Mission with God

Before Class:
Memorize 2 Timothy 2:2 and complete the Bible study.
Read chapters 1, 3 and 4 in *Transforming Discipleship* by Greg Ogden.

Day One – Memorizing God's Word: 2 Timothy 2:2

- 2 Timothy 2:2 is today's memory verse. Read it aloud to yourself and then write it here.

- Now read the verse in context of the surrounding content to better understand its meaning. Read 2 Timothy 1:3 – 14 and 2 Timothy 2:1 – 2.

- Spend some time beginning to memorize the verse.

The Mandate: *Go Make Disciples*

Study It
- How many generations were involved in the process of Timothy's discipleship?

- What were some of the qualities that Timothy, as a disciple maker, had to have? (1 Timothy 2:1–2)

Apply It
- Who is investing in you? Who speaks wisdom into your life?

- Who would say that they walk closer to God because of you? Who is your disciple?

MEN WITH NO REGRETS   Beginning Your Mission with God

Day Two – Supplemental Reading

Read the Introduction and chapters 1, 3 and 4 in the book, *Transforming Discipleship* by Greg Ogden. Do a chapter a day for days Two - Four. Take notes in the space provided.

Greg Odgen is a retired executive pastor of discipleship at Christ Church of Oakbrook in Oakbrook, Illinois. He previously served as Academic Director of the Doctor of Ministry program at Fuller Theological Seminary in Pasadena, California. Author of five discipleship books, Greg now lives out his passion of speaking, teaching, and writing about the disciple-making mission of the church.

Chapter One:

• Notes from the Reading:

• Key Principles and Observations:

• What Challenged you most from the Reading?

The Mandate: *Go Make Disciples*

Day Three – Supplemental Reading

Chapter Three:
- Notes from the Reading:

- Key Principles and Observations:

- What Challenged you most from the Reading?

Day Four – Supplemental Reading

Chapter Four:
- Notes from the Reading:

- Key Principles and Observations:

- What Challenged you most from the Reading?

Day Five – Optional: A Time of Personal Reflection

- Who has positively influenced your journey with Jesus?

- What qualities do these people possess that enabled them to have such an influence on you?

- What qualities is God putting to use in your life to make you influential to those in your world?

- What characteristics remain in your life that hinder you from being used by God to influence your world?

- So often when it comes to ministering to others, we look at the structures and strategies of the church and ask how we fit into what is already happening. While this is not wrong, it may be providing too comfy a box for you – inside which you do not truly ask God to reveal His plans for your life. With that caution in mind, do you sense God's pull in your life to engage in anything new at this time?

- Spend time in prayer for the workers that God has used to bring you to this point in your faith journey. Pray the Lord of the harvest will send workers into His harvest field. Pray to know where you fit into the answer to that prayer.

In Class

Open in Prayer

Memory Verse Review – 2 Timothy 2:2

Small Group Sharing, Accountability and Prayer – 40 minutes
- How has God spoken to you this week, either through His Word or another way?

- Share with your group the person who has had the greatest influence on your spiritual growth as a man.

- Pray for one another, especially as it relates to whom God desires you to invest in.

Large Group Discussion – 40 minutes
- Discuss Transforming Discipleship.
  - How do the seven marks of a healthy church as described in chapter 1 resonate with you? Do you agree with Ogden's definition of reality in the church today?
  - In chapter three, Ogden says that "Jesus lived with the urgency of a three year time line." How would our lives be different if we approached it that way? What would that look like?
  - In chapter four, Ogden explains the four stages that Jesus walked the disciples through. How have you seen this played out in your No Regrets experience, and where would you say you are?

- How does the principle of multiplication differ from the way the church often operates today? Do you think there is an appropriate emphasis on intentional disciple making in the church today?

- Can the typical hectic lifestyle of an American accommodate the cost of disciple making? Each group member should consider whether they have commitments at this time that they must drop or alter to accommodate the calling of disciple making. Share openly, expecting future accountability in this area.

The Mandate: *Go Make Disciples*

- How would you describe the "Master Plan" that characterized Jesus' approach to disciple making?

- Is it possible to be a Bible study "regular" but not a disciple-making participant? Discuss how this disconnect could happen.

With your time coming to a close as a No Regrets group, it is time to discuss what is next for you as a group. During this discussion, keep in mind that every person is different and every group is different, so there are no right or wrong ways of moving forward. Help each other to be discerning, as you have all along your journey together. Here are a couple of scenarios you will, no doubt, already have on your minds. You will have the next several weeks to pray and discuss the options on the next page:

- Become a Permanent Small Group – You may choose to formalize your group as a place of refuge, accountability and continued growth. Each of you will be investing in others outside this group, because multiplying your investment calls you to do this, but you may plan to continue as a group for periodic prayer and study. The key issue here is that each person is engaged somehow in the process of disciple making. Your group exists to keep enriching your spiritual formation and to support the mission each person is called upon to do.

- Invest in a New Group of People – Some of you may choose to get involved in a new small group of people. This could be the time to participate as a leader in a ministry within the church that offers small groups. Being involved with children's or student ministry is a beautiful way of laying the foundation among the most impressionable disciples. It gives new meaning to the phrase "going slow and starting small"! You may choose to start a new No Regrets study with a group of young believers.

- Called Out – Some of you are called to engage in a compassionate ministry somewhere in the community, or perhaps the other side of an ocean. The possibilities are too limitless to name here. Give celebratory commissioning, blessing and financial assistance to your friends who engage in new undertakings.

MEN WITH NO REGRETS   Beginning Your Mission with God

Key Principles

More time spent with fewer people equals greater lasting impact for God.

When a person dies, they live on in two ways: In eternity with Jesus and in the lives of those they influence for Jesus.

Men (his close friends) were the method by which Christ intended to change the world.

You cannot transform the world until you transform a person.

Soon after becoming a Christian in high school, John Slack the man that led me to the Lord, gave me a book entitled, *The Master Plan of Evangelism*. He told me to read it and when I was done we would talk about it. Robert Coleman looks at the life of Jesus and how He disciples men. It is the "Readers Digest" version of *The Training of the Twelve* by A.B. Bruce.

I can honestly say, other than the Bible, no other book has influenced me more in my life and ministry than this little book. Here are a few quotes from it:

> *"One must decide where he wants his ministry to count – in the momentary applause of popular recognition or the reproduction of his life in a few chosen men who will carry on his work after he is gone. Really it is a question of which generation we are living for."*

> *"His concern, speaking of Jesus, was not with programs to reach the multitudes, but with men whom the multitudes would follow."*

> *"The best work is always done with a few. Better to give a year or so to one or two men who learn what it means to conquer for Christ than to spend a lifetime with a congregation just keeping the programs going."*

The Mandate: *Go Make Disciples*

Jesus was never interested in the crowds, but rather spent three years investing in the lives of twelve men. This truly is the Master's Plan. From that point on, I have given my life to investing in a small group of high school students, college students, and now men. Our mandate is quite simple, men to invest our life into the lives of others. As Dawson Trotman, the founder of the Navigators, often said, "Where are your men?" Who are you building into? Next week we are going to examine how you can practically get started.

> *"If you can't reproduce disciples, you can't reproduce leaders. If you can't reproduce leaders, you can't reproduce churches. If you can't reproduce churches, you can't reproduce movements."*
>
> – Neil Cole

Want to Learn How to Invest Your Life in Others?
The Training of the Twelve, A.B. Bruce
The Master Plan of Evangelism, Robert Coleman
The Lost Art of Disciple-Making, Leroy Eims
Eternal Impact, Phil Downer
Mobilizing Men, Steve Sonderman

LESSON SEVEN
Practical Principles: How to Invest in Eternity

Goals for the Lesson:
To learn the practical principles for discipling others
To begin to put together a plan for intentionally investing in others

"In my own life, I can recall several of these profoundly influential figures who were strategically used by God to change the course of my life. The first was a man named Walt. Had it not been for Walt, I seriously doubt whether I would have ever become a follower of Jesus Christ. I came from a broken home. My parents were separated before I was born, and neither one paid much attention to my spiritual condition. To put it bluntly, I could have lived, died, and gone to hell without anyone even bothering to care. But Walt cared. He was part of a tiny church in my neighborhood that developed a passion to affect its community for Christ.

Walt's passion was to reach nine- and ten-year-old boys like me with the Gospel. I'll never forget the Saturday morning I met him. I was sprawled out on a Philadelphia sidewalk playing marbles. Suddenly someone was standing beside me. I looked up to see this gangly guy towering over me – all six feet, four inches of him. My mouth sort of dropped open. "Hey, son, how would you like to go to Sunday School?" he asked. That was an unfortunate question. To my mind, anything that had the word "school" in it had to be bad news. So I shook my head no. But Walt was just getting started. "How would you like to play marbles?" he asked, squatting down. Now he was talking my language! "Sure!" I replied, and quickly set up the game. As the best marble player on the block, I felt supremely confident that I could whip this challenger fairly easily.

Would you believe he beat me in every single game! In fact, he captured every marble I had. In the process, he captured my heart. I may have lost a game and a bit of pride that day, but I gained something infinitely more important – the friendship of a man who cared. A big man, an old man, a man who literally came down to my level by kneeling to play a game of marbles. From then on, wherever Walt was, that's where I wanted to be. Walt built into my life over the next several years in a way that marked me forever. He used to take me and the other boys in his Sunday School class hiking. I'll never forget those times. He had a bad heart, and I'm sure we didn't do it any good, running him all over the woods the way we did. But he didn't seem to mind, because he cared. In fact, he was probably the first person to show me unconditional love.

He was also a model of faithfulness. I can't remember a time that he ever showed up to his Sunday School class unprepared. Not that he was the most scintillating teacher in the world. In fact, he had almost no training for that. Vocationally, he worked in the tool and die trade. But he was for real, and he was also creative. He found ways to involve us boys in the learning process – an approach that made a lasting contribution to my own style of teaching.

Overall, Walt incarnated Christ for me. And not only for me, but for thirteen other boys in my neighborhood, nine of whom also came from broken homes. Remarkably, eleven of us went on to pursue careers as vocational Christian workers – which is ironic, given that Walt himself completed school only through the sixth grade. It just goes to show that a man doesn't need a Ph.D. for God to use him to shape another man.

– **Told by Howard Henricks in his book, Building Character In a Mentoring Relationship: As Iron Sharpens Iron by Howard and William Hendricks**

Just the other day while I was driving back from a speaking engagement in Iowa, I was listening to a message by Professor Hendricks on discipleship. I was reminded of this story as well as the incredible influence he has had in my life. I have listened to hundreds of his messages over the years and believe that he has shaped my thinking on discipleship more than anyone. This week we are going to continue our study on the subject and look at the practical principles for investing in others and how we can get started.

Before Class:
Complete the Bible study.
Read chapters 6 – 8 in *Transforming Discipleship* by Greg Ogden.
Work through the "*Defining Discipleship*" Exercise.

Day One – Bible study
When it comes to being a person of influence, there is no greater example than the Lord Jesus. His life was marked by constant interaction and association with people. In his classic book, *The Master Plan of Evangelism,* Robert Coleman asks and answers a valid question about Jesus' approach.

"Why? Why did Jesus deliberately concentrate His life upon comparatively so few people? Had He not come to save the world? With the glowing announcements of John the Baptist ringing in the ears of multitudes, the Master easily could have had an immediate following of thousands if He wanted them. Why did He not then capitalize upon His opportunities to enlist a mighty army of believers to take the world by storm? Surely the Son of God could have adopted a more enticing program of mass recruitment. Is it not rather disappointing that one with all the powers of the universe at His command would live and die to save the world, yet in the end have only a few ragged disciples to show for His labors?

Jesus was a realist. He fully realized the fickleness of depraved human nature as well as the Satanic forces of this world amassed against humanity, and in this knowledge He based His evangelism on a plan that would meet the need. The multitudes of discordant and bewildered souls were potentially ready to follow Him, but Jesus individually could not possibly give them the personal care they needed. His only hope was to get men imbued with His life who would do it for Him. Hence, He concentrated Himself upon those who were to be the beginning of this leadership. Though He did what He could do to help the multitudes, He had to devote Himself primarily to a few men, rather than the masses, in order that the masses could at last be saved. This was the genius of His strategy."

Jesus chose a few men with whom He could build a relationship and in whom He could pour His life so that when He was gone, the multiplication process could carry His work down through the ages. Today you will examine a number of passages where Jesus is interacting with His disciples. He is selecting, associating, affirming, teaching, and building into men who would become the foundation of the church in the years to come. That you and I are here two centuries later as Jesus' disciples proves that His strategy did not fail.

Practical Principles: *How to Invest in Eternity*

- Read through the following passages to learn from Jesus about intentional influencing of others. Highlight a key word for each passage and note the repeated themes or key principles.

Luke 6:12 – 16

Mark 3:14

Mark 1:16 – 17

Matthew 11:28 – 29

Luke 14:25 – 35

Luke 11:1 – 4

Matthew 10:1, 5 – 7

MEN WITH NO REGRETS   Beginning Your Mission with God

Day Two – Read chapter 6 in the book, *Transforming Discipleship* by Greg Ogden.

- Key Principles and Observations:

- What challenged you most from the reading?

- What were your favorite verses or quotes?

Practical Principles: *How to Invest in Eternity*

Day Three – Read chapter 7 in the book, *Transforming Discipleship* by Greg Ogden.

- Key Principles and Observations:

- What challenged you most from the reading?

- What were your favorite verses or quotes?

MEN WITH NO REGRETS Beginning Your Mission with God

Day Four – Read chapter 8 in the book, *Transforming Discipleship* by Greg Ogden.

• Key Principles and Observations:

• What challenged you most from the reading?

• What were your favorite verses or quotes?

Practical Principles: *How to Invest in Eternity*

Day Five – A Time of Personal Reflection

There are a number of definitions of discipleship below. Read through the following definitions and then work through the questions that follow.

Discipleship is the process of bringing people into right relationship with God, and developing them to full maturity in Christ through intentional growth strategies, that they might multiply the entire process in others also. — **Edmund Chan, Senior Pastor, Covenant Evangelical Free Church, Singapore**

An intentional relationship in which we walk alongside other disciples in order to encourage, equip, and challenge one another in love to grow toward maturity in Christ. This includes equipping the disciple to teach others as well. — **Discipleship Essentials, Greg Ogden**

At its core, discipleship is sharing your life with someone less mature in Christ in a way that causes him to grow in his spiritual walk. — **Eternal Impact, Phil Downer**

Discipleship is about the intentional training of people who voluntarily submit to the Lordship of Christ and who want to become imitators of Him in every thought, word and deed. It will involve teaching, training, experiences, relationships and accountability. It is about being and reproducing spiritually mature zealots for Christ. — **Growing True Disciples, George Barna**

The Commission of Christ to you is to make disciples, not just converts. The object of discipleship is to help young Christians to progress to the point where they are fruitful, mature and dedicated disciples of Christ. — **The Lost Art of Discipleship, Leroy Eims**

- How has the progression of the curriculum of No Regrets and cultivating the life of your small group fostered intentional disciple making? What will keep No Regrets from becoming just another program that men "go through?" What must it be instead?

- Write your own definition for discipleship.

In Class:

Open in Prayer

Memory Verse Review – All verses from this book.

Small Group Sharing, Accountability and Prayer – 40 minutes

- Share any fears that are hindering you from freely engaging with Jesus' calling upon your life.

- Share with the group the names of the men you are looking to ask to invest in.

- Pray for freedom from fear or any sin that entangles you from moving ahead in investing in other's lives right now.

Large Group Discussion – 40 minutes

- Discuss Ogden's book.
  - In your group, discuss what you believe are the main points of the following chapters: *(For example: What was most challenging? What was most helpful? What were you unclear about? What do you want to apply to your group?)*
    – Chapter 6: Life Investment
    – Chapter 7: Multiplication
    – Chapter 8: Transformation

  - How is what you have read in Ogden related to the themes of what you studied in the first three lessons of this study?

- Discuss the definitions of the Discipleship exercise in Day Four.
  - Which definition did each of you resonate with the most?
  - Share with the group the definition that you wrote.

- Finish your time as a group by talking about how you have seen these principles in action the last couple of years. Each man share what discipleship looks like for him in the future.

Practical Principles: *How to Invest in Eternity*

Key Principles
We need a vision to think small.
Disciple making is about relationships; it is not a project but a process.
People are looking for an example to follow, not just words.
People need tangible models of vulnerability, transparency, and accountability.
Effective ministry to others involves interceding, incarnating and making the investment intentionally.

Dorothea Clapp was an obscure lady from Ramsey, New Jersey. She spent most of her life praying for the students at the local high school as they walked past her house on the way to school in the morning. She led a Bible study for the students for many years and invested her life in them. In the early 1950's, Dorothea took a special interest in a young boy named George Verwer. She prayed for him daily and shared with him some tracts from the Gospel of John. She talked to him whenever she had a chance and invited him to a Billy Graham Crusade in New York City. There she prayed with him and led him to the Lord. She then spent time teaching him the Bible, helping him to memorize scripture and to distribute Bible literature. She would often take him to New York City to hand out literature to people walking by.

George Verwer was on fire for God. He later founded a ministry called *Operation Mobilization*, with the objective of getting Bibles and Christian literature into hard-to-reach countries. Today, there are thousands of workers worldwide spreading the Gospel of Jesus Christ into some of the most hardened and impenetrable countries of the world.

In November of 1989, at the age of 88, Dorothea Clapp passed from this life into eternity. But the investment she made in a young high school student continues to multiply, compound and expand in the lives of others around the world. Dorothea lives on in two ways: in eternity with Jesus, and through the legacy of the high school students, George Verwer included, that she influenced for Jesus.

Men, each one of us is going to die at some time, and we are going to each live on in two ways, in eternity with Jesus and in the men and women we influence for Jesus. My question to you is rather simple, "In whose life are you investing your life?"

> *"Only a disciple can make a disciple."*
> – A. W. Tozer

Want to Read More About Being the Church?
The Training of the Twelve, A.B. Bruce
The Master Plan of Evangelism, Robert Coleman
The Lost Art of Disciple Making, Leroy Eims
Eternal Impact, Phil Downer
Mobilizing Men, Steve Sonderman

LESSON EIGHT

Life Plan: The Man with No Regrets

Goals for the Lesson:
To reflect on what God has done over the course of the last two years in your life and the life of your small group
To finalize a plan for moving forward individually and as a group
To celebrate what God has done in your life and in the lives of those in your group

In Al Ries' book, *Focus*, the introduction begins with these lines:

"The sun is a powerful source of energy. Every hour the sun washes the earth with billions of kilowatts of energy. Yet with a hat and some sunscreen, you can bathe in the light of the sun for hours at a time with few ill effects. A laser is a weak source of energy. A laser takes a few watts of energy and focuses them in a coherent stream of light. But with a laser, you can drill a hole in a diamond or wipe out a cancer."

It's all about focus. Without focus we can spend a lot of time and energy running from one activity to the next without effect. The next and final step in your No Regrets experience is to reflect on what God has done in your life and put together a plan for carrying out the things you have incorporated into your life over the last two years, as well as looking to the future and the changes you still want to make.

Whatever God has called you to do, and to be, needs a plan to make it a reality. How many of us have a plan to stay in shape, a plan for when we retire, or a plan for our next vacation? However, it has been found that eight out of ten Christ followers have no plan for spiritual growth. To keep your transformation grounded in reality, you now have the chance to put a plan together that reflects your cooperation with the voice of God directing you into His world.

MEN WITH NO REGRETS Beginning Your Mission with God

Before Class:
Review what God has taught you and how He has transformed your life over the past eight book in the No Regrets Study Series.
Based on what He has done in your life and what He wants you to be and do in the future, put together a plan.

Day One – Reflection on God's Transforming Work in Your Life

Over the course of the last two years you have worked through eight study guides that have intentionally equipped you to be a leader in your home, church, workplace and world. God has hopefully used this process to transform you more into the image of His Son.

For the following reflection time you might want to get those out and page through them to remind yourself of the topics you studied and the work that God did in your heart and life. I have provided a few questions for you to reflect on and to write out some notes.

• Write down one major take-away or challenge from each book:

Book One - Becoming a Follower of Christ

Book Two - Building Your Spiritual Muscle

Book Three - Being the Man God Created You to Be

Book Four - Bringing God to Work with You

MEN WITH NO REGRETS   Beginning Your Mission with God

Day Two – Continued Reflection on God's Transforming Work in Your Life

• Write down one major take-away or challenge from each book:

Book Five - Becoming a Man of Influence

Book Six - Building a Home, Not just a House

Book Seven - Believing and Knowing the Truth

Life Plan: *The Man with No Regrets*

Book Eight - Beginning your Mission with God

Looking back over these questions and the responses you wrote out, here are a couple of overarching questions:

- What benefits have you experienced from being in a group of men for the past two years?

- When you look back at these two years, what are a few major themes you see God working out in your life?

- How have you been equipped to better lead at home, at church, in the workplace and the world?

Day Three and Four – Life Plan for Moving Forward

Your assignment for the next couple of days is to put together a plan for effectively moving forward and finishing strong now that you have completed the No Regrets Study Series. You will be looking at different aspects of your life, reading verses related to them, and answering reflection questions that will help you be specific in making a plan to grow and develop your life.

Ruth Haley Barton, in the wonderful book, *Sacred Rhythms*, says developing a plan for one's life takes time, the counsel of others, and a listening ear to the Spirit. Let all of these influence the ultimate development of your plan. She goes on to say that an effective plan will be characterized by five qualities:

It will be Personal. No two people are the same and no two plans will be the same. Your plan should take into account your unique personality, temperament, season of life, spiritual type, where you are vulnerable to sin, and where you are growing.

It will be Realistic. Consider your life stage and responsibilities. Your plan needs to be something that can realistically be accomplished.

It will be Balanced. If a football player is lifting in the weight room and only works on his arms, he will be of little use on the field. In the same way, as humans, we are complex and our life plan needs to reflect all of the aspects of our life, not just one area.

It will be Flexible. Your plan is not to be a yoke that weighs you down, but a guideline for helping you become what God wants you to be. Every day will be different, and things will come and go. Your plan has to be flexible enough to withstand these changes and interruptions. You may find that, as time goes by, you will need to change your plan to reflect the changes in your life.

It will be Descriptive. Your plan will describe where you are now, the type of spiritual activities you are involved in, as well as where you want to be in the future. It will include what you want to subtract from your life, and what you want to add to your life.

My Plan for Being a No Regrets Man

The Spiritual Disciplines:

1 Timothy 4:7–8: *"Have nothing to do with godless myths and old wives' tales; rather, train yourself to be godly. For physical training is of some value, but godliness has value for all things, holding promise for both the present life and the life to come."*

"A spiritual discipline is any activity we undertake that puts us in closer communion with Christ and His Kingdom." – **Richard Foster, Celebration of Discipline**

- Spiritual Disciplines I have incorporated into my life on a regular basis:

Spiritual Disciplines:	How Often?:

- Spiritual Disciplines I would like to incorporate into my life and how often:

Spiritual Disciplines:	How Often?:

- What schedule changes will I need to make in order to consistently choose these life-giving disciplines?

Relationships:

Ecclesiastes 4:9–10
"Two are better than one, because they have a good return for their work: If one falls down, his friend can help him up. But pity the man who falls and has no one to help him up!

Proverbs 27:17
"As iron sharpens iron, so one man sharpens another."

Proverbs 17:17
"A friend loves at all times, and a brother is born for adversity."

The quality of your life will be greatly determined by the relationships you develop. As Howard Hendricks said at the 1993 Promisekeepers Conference, 'every man needs three types of men in their lives, a "Paul", "Barnabas" and "Timothy".

- Mentors who advise me – list the mentors you have and need and the areas of your life where they help you. Star the ones you have in place already.

Mentor:	Role they will play:

- If you need to put some in place, when do you want to have that done by?_____

- Partners that accept me – list out the men you are accountable to for your actions and attitudes. If you do not have a group, who can you ask to do this in your life?

- If you need to get some men in place, when do you want to have that done by?_____

- Friends that support me – list the men who are your soulmates in life.

MEN WITH NO REGRETS   Beginning Your Mission with God

Training:

A leadership principle that has served me well over the years is that when you stop learning you stop leading. In this section of your plan, you need to ask the question, what do I need to do in order to better do what God has called me to do?

- Book I want to read and when I want it done by:

- Seminar I want to attend and when I will go by: (parenting, marriage, how to share my faith, finances, etc.)

- Class I need to take and when I will take it by:

Experiences:

Philippians 1:29 *"For it has been granted to you on behalf of Christ not only to believe on him, but also to suffer for him."*

James 1:2 *"Consider it pure joy my brothers whenever you face trials of many kinds, because you know that the testing of your faith develops perseverance."*

One of the greatest ways that God transforms us is in the crucible of life. It was A.W. Tozer that said, *"It is doubtful God can use any of us greatly until we have been hurt deeply."* It is in the daily activities of life that God does His work. Take a minute to answer the following questions:

- Am I:

Worshiping on a regular basis?	Yes - No
Giving with a grateful heart?	Yes - No
Demonstrating compassion for those less fortunate?	Yes - No
Sharing my faith with the lost?	Yes - No
Serving in the local church?	Yes - No
Seeking justice for those with no voice?	Yes - No
Investing my life in the life of others?	Yes - No

- What needs to be built into your life that is not there right now? What might you need to cut out, so you have the margin to build it in?

- What is your plan for this and who is going to hold you accountable for it?

Family:

It has been said that if you want to know whether you are living out your Christian faith just ask a man's spouse, and kids, they will tell you! I know mine will. While we have plans for our finances, job and golf game, rarely do we have a plan for our marriage and family. Take a few minutes to develop a plan for moving forward in these relationships.

Spouse:

- How can I best express love to my spouse? What is her love language?

- How can I best nurture my spouse emotionally, relationally, spiritually, and intellectually?

- What is my plan to ensure that I spend quality time relating deeply to my spouse?

Children:
- How can I make my children feel loved and appreciated?

- How can I be my child's cheerleader?

- What is my plan for their development as a person?

Parents:
- What is the best way to convey love to my parents?

- Are there any unresolved issues I need to address with my parents?

MEN WITH NO REGRETS   Beginning Your Mission with God

In Class:

Open in Prayer

Memory Verse Review – Each man share his favorite memory verse from the past two years.

Large Group Discussion – 40 minutes
You will be staying together for the entire time today to celebrate what God has done in each of your lives.

- Watch Video message *You've Finished the Race* by Steve Sonderman

- Take time to finalize what you are going to do as a group after this lesson. You started the discussion in lesson five, and hopefully are in agreement of what is next, but if you have not finished the discussion, take time now to discuss it.

- Each person in your group shares how God has transformed them for His kingdom purposes over the course of the No Regrets experience. The sharing should revolve around the following themes:
  · Where have you seen yourself transformed by God in the last two years?
  · How has God prepared you to influence others for His kingdom purposes? Share where you sense God calling you to join Him in His mission for the world.
  · What are you most thankful for, as a result of your No Regrets experience?

- After each person shares, give them the option to have the group lay hands on and pray for them.
  Spend time in prayers of :
  · Thanksgiving for God's faithfulness in their life.
  · For the ministry to which God is calling them.
  · For anything else they would request prayer for.
  · For them to live a life of No Regrets.

- When every man has shared and been prayed for, you might want to read this statement together and vow to be a part of the Fellowship of the Unashamed. This statement was written by a young pastor in Zimbabwe who had been martyred for his faith. The document was found in his study days after being killed.

Life Plan: *The Man with No Regrets*

"I am part of the Fellowship of the Unashamed. I have the Holy Spirit's power. The die has been cast and I've stepped over the line. The decision has been made. I am a disciple of His. I won't look back, let up, slow down, back away, or be still. My past is redeemed. My present makes sense. My future is secure. I'm finished and done with low living, sight walking, smooth knees, colorless dreams, tamed visions, worldly talking, cheap giving and dwarfed goals. I no longer need preeminence, prosperity, position, promotions, plaudits, or popularity. I don't have to be right, first, tops, recognized, praised, regarded or rewarded. I now live by faith, lean in His presence, walk by patience, I'm uplifted by prayer and labor with power. My pace is set, my gait is fast. My goal is heaven and my road is narrow. My way is rough, my companions are few, my guide is reliable and my mission is clear. I cannot be bought, compromised, detoured, lured away, turned back, deluded, or delayed. I will not flinch in the face of sacrifice, hesitate in the presence of the enemy, pander at the pool of popularity, or meander in the maze of mediocrity. I am a disciple of the Messiah. I must go until He comes, speak of all I know of Him and work until He stops me. And when He comes for His own, by the grace of God, He will have no problem recognizing me, because my colors are clear." – **Unknown Zimbabwean Pastor**

Guys, I want to congratulate you for completing the series. There are lots and lots of men around this country who started, but did not finish. And as we have talked about throughout this study, it is not how you start that matters, but how you finish the race that matters. At the end of his life the apostle Paul said in 2 Timothy 4:7, "I have fought the good fight, I have finished the race, I have kept the faith."

I don't know about you, but I want to do the same. I want to be more in love with Jesus at the end of my life than I am today. I want to be more of a fearless influencer of society tomorrow, than I am today. I want to get to the end of my life and look in the rear view mirror with No Regrets. Our prayer is that as you are now unleashed into the world to live out God's mission for your life, you would know the peace, presence and power of our Lord and Savior Jesus Christ.

It's gametime, so go get them.

No Regrets Study Series
Small Group Resources

No Regrets Small Group Covenant

In order to grow in my discipleship with Christ and to build authentic Christian community, I agree to the following standards:

1. **Total and Complete Confidentiality**
   What I hear here, see here, and say here stays here. I will say nothing that may be traced back or that could be injurious or embarrassing to my group members. My group leader will refer me to a pastor if I am contemplating harming myself or doing harm to others.
2. **Share My Life**
   I will be as open about my life as I can. I will be vulnerable with you, letting you know who I am as a person.
3. **Unconditional Love**
   I will love you and affirm you no matter what you have said or done in the past. I will love you as you are and for what Christ desires you to be.
4. **Voluntary Accountability**
   I will ask the group to hold me accountable for specific areas of my life. With my permission, you can ask me about the goals I set with God, my family, personal life, and world. I expect you to lovingly not "let me off the hook." "As iron sharpens iron, so one man sharpens another." (Proverbs 27:17). On the basis of this verse, I ask you to please share with me any areas in my life that do not reflect Jesus, because I want to grow in personal holiness.
5. **Pray for One Another**
   I promise to pray for those in my group regularly and lift their needs to the Lord.
6. **Sensitivity to Where People Are**
   I understand each man in this group is at a different point in his walk with the Lord. I will accept you the way you are, but encourage you to grow in the Lord. I will seek to create a safe environment where people can be heard and loved.
7. **Spiritual Growth**
   I will come prepared with my work completed and my verses memorized each week. I will set aside 10–15 minutes for a daily time with God. I will make every effort to be at class; it will have high priority in my schedule. If I cannot attend, I will call my leader to let him know. I will commit to being a Minister for Jesus.

I view my participation in No Regrets as a means of preparing myself for a life of ministry wherever Jesus may take me. From the beginning of the study, I will look for others to invest my life in and minister to.

Signed:_____ Date:_____

Small Group Roles

Leader This role will already be filled as the group begins. Leads the small group through the series and helps facilitate the group discussion.

Leader–in–Training Responsible for assisting the leader and running the group when the leader is unavailable. Ideally this will be someone who is interested in leading his own group one day.

On–Time Coordinator Responsible for starting and finishing the components of the meeting on time.

Food Coordinator Responsible for coordinating refreshments if the group decides that food is going to be part of each meeting.

Social Coordinator Responsible for planning whatever social events your group wishes to have. We encourage you to get together socially as soon as possible after No Regrets has started, as this ignites relationships between those members who are new to each other. Consider inviting spouses to such gatherings. Potlucks in somebody's home are great ways to share life together.

Communications Coordinator Responsible for keeping the group informed about any news, upcoming meetings and social events.

Service Project Coordinator Responsible for planning and carrying out a service project during the eight weeks of the study. This is a chance for team members to impact their community together. We have found that when people work together on a project, no matter what it is, it helps bring unity to the group. Leaders should talk to their pastors and church leaders regarding possible service projects in their community.

Memory Verse Master Responsible to come prepared each week to quiz the participants on their memory verses. It is important for this person to focus on the verse for the current week and periodically quiz the members on all of the verses memorized to date. The spiritual discipline of Scripture memory opens the door for God to work in so many ways. A creative quizmaster can be a key leader to insure that this discipline takes root in everybody's life.

Prayer Warrior Responsible for the creative and compassionate direction of the prayer efforts of the group. Communicate prayer requests, updates and answered prayer via e–mail.

Role Sign-Up

Leader:

Leader in Training:

On Time Coordinator:

Food Coordinator:

Social Coordinator:

Communications Coordinator:

Service Project Coordinator:

Memory Verse Master:

Prayer Warrior:

Spiritual "Vital Signs" Self–Assessment

Infant Have not begun to grow: **1**
Adolescent Some growth: **2**
Adult Mature and well developed in this area of my walk: **3**

Magnifying the Lord

I have incorporated the spiritual disciplines into my life on a regular basis (solitude, silence, prayer, meditation, memorization, Bible reading, journaling, fasting, etc.).
MY VITAL SIGN RATING IS   **1**   **2**   **3**

I strive to surrender all aspects of my life to the Lord (i.e. decisions, relationships, resources) in an attempt to bring Him pleasure.
MY VITAL SIGN RATING IS   **1**   **2**   **3**

I am engaged in regular worship within a church body and within a fellowship of believers.
MY VITAL SIGN RATING IS   **1**   **2**   **3**

I see my giving to the church as an act of worship.
MY VITAL SIGN RATING IS   **1**   **2**   **3**

I am in the habit of confessing my sin on a daily basis and seek to repent of it.
MY VITAL SIGN RATING IS   **1**   **2**   **3**

Maturity in Christ

I see evidence of character development in my life and am becoming more like Christ in thought, word, and deed.
MY VITAL SIGN RATING IS   **1**   **2**   **3**

I have developed the ability to embrace trials and life's obstacles as a means to grow me in perseverance and character, and shape me into dependence on Christ.
MY VITAL SIGN RATING IS   **1**   **2**   **3**

I have developed a plan for spiritual growth that includes building into my life the experiences, activities, and relationships necessary to grow into Christ–likeness.
MY VITAL SIGN RATING IS   **1**   **2**   **3**

My daily choices and decisions are based upon biblical principles and values.
MY VITAL SIGN RATING IS   **1**   **2**   **3**

I am dependent on the work of the Holy Spirit in my life and follow His guidance as I go through the day.
MY VITAL SIGN RATING IS   **1**   **2**   **3**

Ministry

I am in regular prayer over how God would have me multiply what I am learning about discipleship to pass this on to other disciples who will make disciples.
MY VITAL SIGN RATING IS 1 2 3

I understand what my spiritual gifts are and I am seeking to serve God by using them in the context of the local church.
MY VITAL SIGN RATING IS 1 2 3

I am using my resources efficiently (time, talent, treasure) to maximize my impact for the Kingdom of God.
MY VITAL SIGN RATING IS 1 2 3

My heart is sensitive to the plight of the poor and is engaged in helping them.
MY VITAL SIGN RATING IS 1 2 3

I am committed to serving people across the street and around the world.
MY VITAL SIGN RATING IS 1 2 3

Mission

I regularly pray for the salvation of specific non–Christian people I know (family, community, work, school, etc.) for how they can know Jesus Christ in a personal relationship.
MY VITAL SIGN RATING IS 1 2 3

I intentionally develop and maintain relationships with non–Christians with the hope of being able to share my faith with them.
MY VITAL SIGN RATING IS 1 2 3

I effectively share my faith in Jesus Christ with unbelieving people.
MY VITAL SIGN RATING IS 1 2 3

I understand and am able to clearly explain my beliefs to others.
MY VITAL SIGN RATING IS 1 2 3

I am supporting/participating in World Missions.
MY VITAL SIGN RATING IS 1 2 3

Membership

I intentionally and regularly meet with God's family at a church for the purpose of fellowship, encouragement, growth, and accountability.
MY VITAL SIGN RATING IS 1 2 3

I have become a member of a church body to demonstrate my commitment to the Body of Christ.
MY VITAL SIGN RATING IS 1 2 3

When I have offended someone or have been offended, I seek to restore the relationship.
MY VITAL SIGN RATING IS 1 2 3

The words I speak are positive and encouraging and build up the Body of Believers.
MY VITAL SIGN RATING IS 1 2 3

I am willing to be vulnerable and open with those in my discipleship circle. I share my real needs for prayer and am willing to support others in turn.
MY VITAL SIGN RATING IS 1 2 3

Personal Spiritual Conditioning Goals Chart

Personal Goals

Magnifying the Lord
How can I bring pleasure to the Lord through worship as I go about the rhythms of my daily life?

Maturity in Christ
How can I better cooperate with God's work in refining my character to make me look more like Christ?

Ministry
What are my plans to engage in service inside the body of believers as well as outside the church?

Mission
How can I share my faith with those in my circle of influence? Where am I engaged with my resources for the cause of Christ on a local, national and worldwide level?

Membership
How can I cultivate more meaningful interaction with the body of Christ and invest myself in disciple–making?

Come prepared to share with your group as much as you want about your goals.

Accountability Questions

1. How much time did you spend in prayer this week?
2. Did you pray for the others in this group?
3. Did you put yourself in an awkward situation with the opposite sex?
4. At any time did you compromise your integrity?
5. What one sin plagued your walk with God this week?
6. How did you accomplish your spiritual goals this week?
7. Are you giving to the Lord's work financially?
8. How have you demonstrated a servant's heart?
9. Did you treat those in your sphere of influence (peers, neighbors, co–workers, family members etc.) as people loved by God?
10. What significant thing did you do for your spouse and/or family?
11. What was your biggest disappointment? How did you handle it?
12. What was your biggest joy? Did you thank God?
13. What do you see as your #1 need for next week?
14. Are you satisfied with the time you spent with the Lord this week?
15. How did you take time to show compassion for others in need?
16. How did you control your tongue?
17. What did you do this week to enhance your relationship with your spouse?
18. Did you pray and read God's Word this week? What did you derive from this time?
19. In what ways have you launched out in faith since we last met?
20. In what ways has God blessed you this week?
21. What disappointments consumed your thought life this week?
22. Did you observe biblical boundaries in relation to the opposite sex this week, in thought, action, and word?
23. How have you been tempted this week? How did you respond?
24. How has your relationship with Christ been changing?
25. Did you worship in church this week?
26. Have you shared your faith this week? How?
27. What are you wrestling with in your thought life?
28. What have you done for someone else this week?
29. In what ways have you seen the character of Christ formed in you?
30. Where are you depending on God?
31. Are you growing in your love for God and for others?

Chuck Swindoll's Accountability Questions:

1. Have you been with a woman this week in such a way that was inappropriate or could have looked to others that you were using poor judgment?
2. Have you been completely above reproach in all your financial dealings this week?
3. Have you exposed yourself to any explicit material this week?
4. Have you spent daily time in prayer and in the Scriptures this week?
5. Have you fulfilled the mandate of your calling this week?
6. Have you taken time off to be with your family this week?
7. Have you just lied to me?

Scripture Memory Secrets

As you start to memorize a verse:
Read in your Bible the context of the verse.
Try to gain a clear understanding of what the verse actually means. You may want to read it in other Bible translations or paraphrases to get a better grasp of the meaning.
Read the verse several times thoughtfully, aloud or in a whisper. This will help you grasp the verse as a whole. Each time you read it, say the reference, then the verse, then the reference again.
Discuss the verse with God in prayer, and continue to seek his help for success in Scripture memory.

While you are memorizing a verse:
Say the verse aloud as much as possible.
Learn the reference first.
After learning the reference, learn the first phrase of the verse. Once you have learned the reference and first phrase and have repeated them correctly several times, add more phrases one by one.
Think about how the verse applies to you and your daily circumstances.
Always include the reference as part of the verse as you learn and review it. Repeat the reference both before and after the verse.

After you can quote the verse correctly:
You'll find it helpful to write out the verse. This deepens the impression in your mind.
Review the verse immediately after learning it, and repeat it frequently in the next few days. This is crucial for fixing the verse firmly in mind, because of how quickly we tend to forget something we've recently learned.
REVIEW! REVIEW! REVIEW! Repetition is the best way to engrave the verses on your memory.

How to review memory verses with someone else:
Follow this procedure: If the memory verses are written on cards, one person holds the other person's verse cards and reads the reference of the first card (if the verses aren't written out, just use the Bible). The other person then repeats the reference and goes on to quote the entire verse, with the reference again at the end. Then go on to other verses in the same way. First review the memory verses you know best.

Quote your verses clearly and not too rapidly so you can be easily understood.

Make it your goal to repeat each verse word perfectly.

While the other person is quoting his verses, be helpful and encouraging. Do all you can to ensure his success.

When the other person makes a mistake, signal this to him by shaking your head or saying no. Give him verbal help only if he asks you.

Once the other person has realized his mistake, have him repeat the entire verse word perfectly before going on. (Memorizing and reviewing Scripture with one or more friends will provide mutual encouragement, as well as opportunities to discuss difficulties in memorization. You will also be helped by having someone with whom to share how God is using the verses in your life.)

Two essentials in Scripture memory:

Two rules form the foundation for a successful Scripture memory program:

Consistently memorize new verses each week.

Follow a daily program of reviewing the verses you have already memorized.

If memorizing Scripture becomes too routine:

Don't get discouraged if your Scripture memory work begins to seem too routine. The process of recording Scripture on your mind and heart does have a mechanical aspect. It requires certain methods and a great deal of perseverance. But as long as the process of imprinting God's word on your heart is moving forward, these Scripture verses will be continually available for life–giving work.

There are helpful things you can do, however, if your Scripture memory program begins to seem lifeless. Try spending more time going over your verses in prayer and meditation. Also begin using the verses in your conversations or in letters. New freshness can come through sharing Scripture with others.

Keep in mind that memorizing and meditating on Scripture is a practical way of making them available to the Holy Spirit to use in your life.

For more information and teaching on memorization, go to: www.memoryverses.org

Materials taken from the Topical Memory System. Copyright 1969, 1981 by The Navigators.
Used by permission of NavPress, Colorado Springs, CO. All rights reserved.

Guidelines for Reading Old Testament History

History is the most common type of literature found in the Bible (over 40 percent of the Old Testament). The following books are primarily historical: Genesis, Exodus, Numbers, Deuteronomy, Joshua, Judges, Ruth, 1 & 2 Samuel, 1 & 2 Kings, 1 & 2 Chronicles, Ezra, Nehemiah, and Esther. The historical writers attempted to present a reliable record of past events. History shows how God has chosen to enter our fallen world to speak with us. The writings glorify Him, help us to understand and appreciate Him, and give us a picture of His providence and protection. Remember that God is the leading character in all the Old Testament historical books.

It will help you as you read Old Testament history to realize that the story is being told in effect, on three levels. The top level is that of the whole universal plan of God worked out through His creation. Key aspects of the plot at this top level are the initial creation, the fall of humanity (as a result of sin), the need for salvation, and the promise of redemption through the coming Messiah (Jesus Christ). The middle level centers on Israel: the call of Abraham, the establishment of Patriarchs, the slavery in Egypt, God's deliverance from bondage and the conquest of the Promised Land, Israel's frequent sins and increased disloyalty, God's patient protection and pleading with them, the destruction of northern Israel and later Judah, and the restoration of the people after the Exile. Then there is the bottom level. Here are found all the hundreds of individual stories that make up the other two levels. Some examples include the story of Joseph (Gen. 37 – 50) and the story of David's adultery with Bathsheba (2 Sam. 11 – 12). You will not fully do justice to an individual story unless you recognize its part within the other two levels.

The historical writers not only made decisions about what to include, they also interpreted the events. As with all Scripture, historical writers were inspired by God. Look for the motivating questions and issues that drove the human author of the book you are studying.

Look for the example the historical account provides. The biblical authors recount the events of history to teach their contemporary generations and future ones about God and about life (cf. 1 Cor. 10:6). In some cases we have to find the significance for our lives ourselves; in other cases, the biblical author reveals that significance to us. Ask yourself: How do I relate to these people? In what ways do I experience the same hopes and fears, similar desires and motivations? What could God be telling me through their stories? What changes in attitude or action will I attempt as a result?

We need to exercise some caution as we think about contemporary application of Old Testament stories. We can't assume that everything recorded is an example given for us to our spiritual growth. We must take into account that some events in the past occurred under special circumstances and no longer apply to us. For example, the "holy wars" fought by Joshua to take control of the Promised Land are unique to the Old Testament when the people of God were one nation. Today the people of God are scattered among many nations and our holy war is now a spiritual conflict, not a physical one (see Eph. 6:10 – 20). The best safeguard against misapplying historical material is to find support from a passage that teaches the principle in a straightforward manner.

Always look for the connection to Christ. He is the center of history according to the Bible. All the events of the Old Testament anticipate the great redemption Jesus performed on the cross. The Bible (including the Old Testament) is one story. All the different stories, including those of Abraham, Moses, David, and Nehemiah, contribute to the single story of God's salvation, and that story climaxes with Jesus Christ.

For more information on how to read Old Testament History, see Reading the Bible with Heart and Mind by Longman, pp. 97–112; or How to Read the Bible for All Its Worth, by Fee and Stuart, pp. 78–93.

MEN WITH NO REGRETS Bringing God to Work with You

Small Group Prayer Requests – Lesson 1

"Do not be anxious about anything, but in everything, by prayer and petition, with thanksgiving, present your requests to God."
Philippians 4:6

Small Group Prayer Requests – Lesson 2

Small Group Prayer Requests – Lesson 3

"Answer me when I call to you, O my righteous God. Give me relief from my distress; be merciful to me and hear my prayer."

Psalm 4:1

Small Group Prayer Requests – Lesson 4

Small Group Prayer Requests – Lesson 5

"Do not be anxious about anything, but in everything, by prayer and petition, with thanksgiving, present your requests to God."
Philippians 4:6

Small Group Prayer Requests – Lesson 6

Small Group Prayer Requests - Lesson 7

"Answer me when I call to you, O my righteous God. Give me relief from my distress; be merciful to me and hear my prayer."
Psalm 4:1

Small Group Prayer Requests - Lesson 8

NO REGRETS MEN'S MINISTRIES

Partnering with Church Leaders.

Many men will come to the end of their life, look in the rear view mirror and see a long list of regrets. We partner with local church leadership, helping them to initiate intentional men's ministry that transforms hearts, not just behavior. We are passionate about helping more men live life on purpose with No Regrets.

No Regrets Men's Conference
Host A Live Broadcast.

No Regrets Men's Conference is a live one-day event equipping men to live as fully-devoted, sold-out, all-in followers of Christ. Join with thousands of other men in churches across the nation via live high definition video stream the first Saturday in February. We stream the music, speakers, and other life-changing content. You choose to pick up the entire day or add your own live seminars and music. It's literally plug and play. Plus, No Regrets isn't just a one-day, mountaintop experience. Following the No Regrets Men's Conference event, our new No Regrets Study Series will help you to generate more small groups to connect and disciple your men for the other 364 days a year.

Want more details?
Watch our new Host Site Video on our website!

www.menwithnoregrets.org

www.menwithnoregrets.org · 800-919-9059
No Regrets Men's Ministries · 777 S. Barker Road · Brookfield, WI 53045

NO REGRETS MEN'S MINISTRIES

Ministry Building Resources

Mobilizing Men for One–on–One Ministry
Steve Sonderman

This is a book for every man who desires to follow after Christ. While not every man is called to be a pastor, each is called to have an authentic ministry to men. It's true. Every man is called to walk along side his brothers to make Christ known. Learn how to minister to the men around you through real relationships and one–on–one disciple making. Not only will this book help each man grow up spiritually, it will develop more men for your church ready to answer the call "to disciple men who disciple men who disciple men".

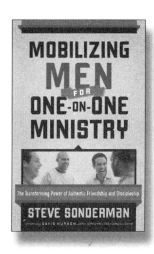

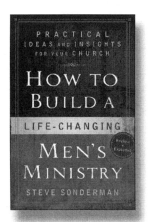

How to Build a Life–Changing Men's Ministry
Steve Sonderman

Written for pastors, church and lay leaders responsible for ministry to men, find the inspiration and practical ideas you need to take your ministry, to the next level and beyond. Today with men leaving the church in droves, more than ever before, it's time to reach out to men with intentional ministry designed specifically for them. So whether you are starting a men's ministry from scratch, or wanting to breathe new life into an established program, this is the book to help you develop the leadership team you'll need to move forward.

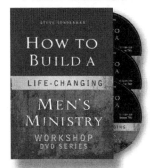

How to Build a Life – Changing Men's Ministry DVD Series
Steve Sonderman teaches this series of 10 DVD's, engaging men's ministry teams, around the world, to move their ministry to men forward.

www.menwithnoregrets.org • 800-919-9059
No Regrets Men's Ministries • 777 S. Barker Road • Brookfield, WI 53045

NO REGRETS CONFERENCE

Nationwide Men's Conference.

Every Year – First Saturday in February

Held annually on the first Saturday of February. This conference for men was created to meet each man where they are and to challenge them to move deeper into relationship with Jesus. A one-day event featuring nationally known speakers, multiple break-out seminars on the life-changing issues men face today, this conference encourages men to find purpose and live with No Regrets.

Host the No Regrets Conference at your local church by live video stream.

We stream the music, speakers, and other life changing content. You choose to pick up the entire day or add your own live seminars and music. Visit www.menwithnoregrets.org.

Take No Regrets Home.

Can't come to the Conference? Want to relive the experience or share with others? No Regrets Conference DVD sets are now available! For ordering information, just visit www.menwithnoregrets.org

2011
Rock Solid

2012
Unleashed

2013
Transformed

www.menwithnoregrets.org · 800-919-9059
No Regrets Men's Ministries · 777 S. Barker Road · Brookfield, WI 53045

NO REGRETS STUDY SERIES

Change the Course of Your Life.

Intro
Beginning the Race

Start a Small Group for Beginners and get men ready for the race of their lifetime.

Not just another light-on-content, men's small group study, this disciple making program is designed to model, teach, and encourage practical application of biblical principles that build a foundation for living life in Christ. Men learn what it means to be a real disciple of Jesus, how to follow after Jesus, how to pray for others, encourage one-another, forgive one-another and love one-another. They will prepare to find their Kingdom purpose becoming empowered to serve as the "hands and feet" of Jesus at home, in church, on the job and in the community where they live. This program is a series of (8) 8-week Bible studies that a typical small group of men complete over a two-year period. (Year One: Books 1-4; Year Two: Books 5-8). The *Beginning the Race* book, a six-week study, is designed to be used as either a group study book in itself or a kick-start to the No Regrets Study Series.

Book 1:
Becoming a Fully-Devoted Follower of Christ

Discover how to follow after Jesus and find your Kingdom purpose.

Book 2:
Building Your Spiritual Muscle

Explore the spiritual disciplines God uses to train and work out His team.

Book 3:
Being the Man God Created You to Be

Learn how God defines masculinity and become the man He created you to be.

Book 4:
Bringing God to Work with You

Study how to keep your integrity, find balance and serve others on the job.

Book 5:
Becoming a Man of Influence

Identify your spiritual gifts and create change as a servant leader.

Book 6:
Building a Home, Not Just a House

Explore practical tools for growing your marriage and parenting your children.

Book 7:
Believing and Knowing the Truth

Solidify your faith as you learn the reasons why-to-believe what-you-believe.

Book 8:
Beginning Your Mission with God

Prepare to understand God's plans to use you to expand and train His team.

www.menwithnoregrets.org • 800-919-9059
No Regrets Men's Ministries • 777 S. Barker Road • Brookfield, WI 53045

one day, multiple sites
one purpose

Jumpstart your annual ministry to men on the first Saturday of every February with the No Regrets Conference. It's a national day of ministry reaching out to men right in their local church. Host the event via live streaming and join with thousands of men from around the country, gathering on one day to bring glory to God.

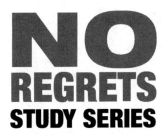

for the other 364 days

Not just another light-on-content, men's small group study, this disciple making program is designed to model, teach, and encourage practical application of biblical principles that build a foundation for living life in Christ. This program is a series of (8) 8-week Bible studies that a typical small group of men complete over a two-year period.

**EMPOWERING MEN TO LIVE
WITH PURPOSE AND NO REGRETS**

In 1904 William Borden graduated from a Chicago high school. As heir to a dairy fortune, he was already wealthy. For his high school graduation present, his parents gave 16-year-old Borden a trip around the world. As the young man traveled through Asia, the Middle East, and Europe, he felt a growing burden for the world's hurting people. Finally, Bill Borden wrote home about his "desire to be a missionary." One friend expressed disbelief that Bill was "throwing himself away as a missionary." In response, Borden wrote two words in the back of his Bible: **NO RESERVES**

When he returned from his travels, Borden went to Yale University where he led Bible studies, and volunteered whenever he could. His motto during his college years was "Say 'no' to self and 'yes' to Jesus every time." Upon graduation from Yale, Borden turned down high-paying job offers. In his Bible, he wrote two more words: **NO RETREATS**

Borden went on to do graduate work at Princeton Seminary, and then promptly set sail for China. At a stopover in Egypt, he contracted spinal meningitis. Within a month, 25-year-old William Borden was dead. Was Borden's untimely death a waste? Not in God's perspective. Prior to his death, Borden had written two more words in his Bible. Underneath the words "No Reserves" and "No Retreats," he had written: **NO REGRETS**

WILLIAM BORDEN, 1887–1913

Excerpted from "Borden of Yale" by Moody Press.
Visit us at menwithnoregrets.org